# BLUE ANGELS

## 50 Years of Precision Flight

Nicholas A. Veronico & Marga B. Fritze

MBI Publishing Company

# Dedication

*This book is dedicated to all of the professional men and women who have worked so hard, and sometimes paid the ultimate price, to forge the reputation of the Blue Angels.*

*For Kimberly and Mark.*
*To the glories of the past, the challenges of the present, and the excitement of the future.*

*In memory of Carl Fritze*
*and for the Blue Angels—who got me into this crazy business in the first place.*

First published in 1996 by MBI Publishing Company, PO Box 1, 729 Prospect Avenue, Osceola, WI 54020-0001 USA

MBI Publishing Company books are also available at discounts in bulk quantity for industrial or sales-promotional use. For details write to Special Sales Manager at Motorbooks International Wholesalers & Distributors, 729 Prospect Avenue, PO Box 1, Osceola, WI 54020-0001 USA.

Library of Congress Cataloging-in-Publication Data

Veronico, Nick.
     Blue Angels : 50 years of precision flight /
     Nicholas A. Veronico, Marga B. Fritze.
          p.  cm.
Includes bibliographical references and index.
ISBN 0-7603-0138-7 (pbk. : alk. paper)
1. United States. Naval Flight Demonstration Squadron—History. I. Fritze, Marga B. II. Title.
VG94.6.N38V37     1996
797.5'4—dc20               96-716

*On the front cover (main):* Blue Angels, Diamond Pass, smoke on. How many hundreds of thousands of rolls of film are shot of the Blue Angels each year? *Armand Veronico (inset):* Voris in a serious pose in the cockpit of the F8F. Voris, over 6 feet tall, would wear out the shoulders of his flying suits in the narrow cockpit. *Voris collection*

*On the frontispiece:* The Number 1 Phantom taxis out in preparation for a formation takeoff. With their two huge afterburning engines, Phantoms waste no time getting airborne. *Wayne McPherson Gomes*

*On the title page:* Rare and unusual photo of all Blue Angel aircraft types on board the USS *Kearsarge* (CVA-33). From left, Grumman F8F Bearcat, Grumman F9F-5 Panther, Grumman F9F-8 Cougar, and Grumman F11F Tiger. *John M. Campbell collection*

*On the back cover (top):* The Blue Angels at Grumman's Bethpage factory accepting a factory-fresh F8F-1. From left: May, Wickendoll, Voris, Knight. *Vorris collection* **(bottom):** The TA-4J flown by the team's public affairs officer. *John M. Campbell collection*

Printed in China

# Contents

| | Acknowledgments | 6 |
| | Introduction | 7 |
| Chapter One | The Birth of the Blues: "Get It Up, Get It On, Get It Down" | 9 |
| Chapter Two | Bearcats to Panther Jets | 19 |
| Chapter Three | Restarting the Team After Korea | 33 |
| Chapter Four | Enter the Cougar | 47 |
| Chapter Five | The Blue Angels Go Supersonic | 53 |
| Chapter Six | Phantoms: Raw Power, Tragic Team Member | 69 |
| Chapter Seven | Rebuilding the Team with "Good Solid Airmanship and Good Solid Maneuvers" | 79 |
| Chapter Eight | The F/A-18 Hornet Years (1986 to Present) | 95 |
| Chapter Nine | Behind the Scenes with the Blue Angels | 103 |
| | Appendices | |
| Appendix I | Aircraft Specifications and Bureau Numbers | 120 |
| Appendix II | Roster of Officers, 1946–95 | 124 |
| | Index | 128 |

# Acknowledgments

Like anything worthwhile, this project has encompassed several years of planning, research, and interviews. We have been fortunate to receive the gracious assistance of so many who have been willing to pass on what they know. We would like to issue special thanks to Blue Angels Ed McKellar and Zeke Cormier who gave us the idea in the first place, as well as their time and access to their files; to a number of Blue Angels who gave generously of their time, recollections, and photographs, including Butch and Thea Voris, Zeke and Kitty Cormier, Jake and Jeanne Robcke, E. L. "Whitey" Feightner, Ed Holley, Ray Hawkins, Ken Wallace, Bill Wheat, Tony Less, G. R. "Bear" Smith, and John Kirby; Harry Gann and Jay Hubbard of the Hubbard Historical Center for their knowledge, kindness, and unwavering support, as well as research materials; George Kirkman of the Santa Monica Museum of Flight; Ray Wagner of the San Diego Aerospace Museum for historical research materials and for being there to answer questions; William and Tilley Larkins; Harrison W. Rued; Ron Strong; Ed Davies; Wayne McPherson Gomes; John Campbell; Karen Haack; A. Kevin Grantham; Armand Veronico; Pamela Veronico; Kim Tamez; Mark Dentone; Milo Peltzer; Scott Thompson; Robert Kropp; Todd Hackbarth; Betty Anderson; and Thomas Wm. McGarry.

We also received valuable assistance from Karen James, Museum of Naval Aviation; Larry A. Feliu, Grumman History Center; Georgia Engle, Northrop/Grumman (Vought Aircraft); Bill Valenti, NAS Alameda Public Affairs; and H. "Ace" Campbell and Lindy Hollingsworth of the American Aviation Historical Society.

Our thanks also to the members of VMFAT-101 at MCAS El Toro for their gracious cooperation, Michael Haenggi and Motorbooks International, Judy Semler for her help in getting this project off the ground, and to Beryl Fritze, for always believing.

—*Marga Fritze and Nicholas A. Veronico*

# Introduction

Hundreds of millions of people have watched the Navy's elite Blue Angels in awe over the past 50 years. The blue and the gold celebrate their golden anniversary in 1996, capping 50 years of glory. We have watched them fly, now it's time to hear their stories. Combined with current and historic photographs, the story of the Blue Angels unfolds.

A blending of the humorous and the serious, team members describe what it was like to be a Blue Angel and what happened during their tenures. Presented chronologically, this book is also presented by type of aircraft flown (e.g., Hellcat, Panther, Skyhawk, and so on). The aircraft reflect the state of aviation's exponential development in the twentieth century and, along with the often colorful personalities involved, have been one of the primary determinants in shaping the Blue Angel show as it is today.

This book is a fusion of text and pictures. It is not meant to be yet another unopened book gathering dust on America's coffee tables, but a fascinating, readable book using vibrant illustrations that often tell stories of their own.

Today, there are nearly 300 airshows a year across the United States. Of those, the Blue Angels fly in nearly 120 cities every season. Given the recent interest in America's military involvement in Operations Desert Shield and Desert Storm, it is a rare person who hasn't heard of the team, if not having actually seen them in action. The team's visibility is enormous. The Marine Corps Air Station El Toro Air Show, for example, in southern California, draws crowds numbering more than 1.5 million over a single weekend, outdrawing almost every professional sport. One of the biggest reasons for such high attendance is that the Blue Angels are often the star attraction.

What is it about the team that makes it so popular? It doesn't matter how many times you've seen the team in action, the thrill of watching six jets working in perfect harmony or feeling the vibrations running through your body as the solo pilots blast overhead never seems to fade. For another, there is a guarantee of a quality performance—no one leaves disappointed after watching the Blue Angels perform. Here, also, is the rare chance to see what civilians so rarely get a glimpse of—the defenders of our nation in their "office," an afterburning jet screaming through the sky. Their jets seem just a little cleaner, their salutes a little snappier, and their job just a little more glamorous. But it is also the intangible—the myths, legends, traditions, and standards—that make the squadron what it is.

Prior to transitioning into the Bearcat, the team had grown
to five members, left to right: Taddeo, Stouse, Voris,
Wickendoll, Cassidy.
*Voris collection*

# Chapter One

# The Birth of the Blues: "Get It Up, Get It On, Get It Down"

The Navy, anxious to keep up with the US Army Air Corps, made several early attempts to form a flight demonstration team in the mid-1920s. Continuing until the outbreak of World War II, it was a colorful and exciting period, full of experimentation and innovation. Taking wing in the mid- to late-1920s for an aviation-starved public, the early military demonstration teams were fairly low on bureaucratic structure and high on thrills. Seeing groups of planes flying while roped together was not an uncommon sight. Few teams lasted more than a year or two, but many of the team members went on to fly with new teams. Aircraft, mostly biplanes, were being improved and upgraded continuously, but many of the principles learned in these early experiments in precision aerobatics are still practiced today.

## Early Air Shows

The first airshow ever held is widely acknowledged to be the Reims, France, Air Meet in August 1909. Some of aviation's most illustrious names gathered: Bleriot, Santos-Dumont, Voisin. Other European shows quickly followed, such as those at Blackpool and London, England; Leopardstown, Ireland; Lanark, Scotland; and Berlin, Germany.

The first airshow west of the Mississippi took place January 10–20, 1910, on ranch property near Los Angeles, California. Among the famous names involved in the Dominguez Hills event were promoter Harry Chandler (of the Los Angeles *Times*) and Glen Curtiss, who was a participant and set a new world record with a passenger on board (55 mph). It was around this time that the Navy was starting to believe that aircraft might be used in battle (their colleagues in the US Army had already established an aeronautical division in the Army Signal Corps back in 1907). In 1912, the Navy was the first (of many) to stage a simulated dogfight and even a night show. Some of the more unusual events included a "marriage in aeroplane" and a "race contested by man, beast, motorcycle, automobile, and aeroplane."

## Post-World War I

After a break in military demonstration flying caused by the intervention of the Great War (World War I, 1914–18), military commanders were soon approving requests for performances because the military was already recognizing the public relations value of such events. It probably reached its peak on November 25, 1918, in San Diego, California, with a fly-over of more than 200 aircraft.

The first picture ever taken of the Navy's Flight Exhibition Team in flight. The May 30, 1946, photo is of poor quality but is extremely rare. Butch Voris said, "We didn't do a lot of photography in the early days. We hadn't made our name yet, and we never thought what this thing would be like 50 years down the road. At the time, we were just trying to get up and down, let alone think so far in advance." When in the three-plane vee formation, Voris flew lead in No. 1, Lt. M. N. "Wick" Wickendoll as right wing in No. 2, and Lt. (j.g.) M. W. "Mel" Cassidy as left wing in No. 3. *Voris collection*

## Enter the Three Sea Hawks

One of the early teams included the Three Sea Hawks, trained by D. W. "Tommy" Tomlinson, who described his life first as a gypsy flyer and his work in forming the Navy's first official demonstration team in an autobiography titled appropriately, *The Sky's The Limit.* In terms of Navy demonstration teams, Tomlinson was its godfather.

Attending the 1927 National Air Races at Spokane, Washington, as a civilian spectator, Tomlinson watched Army aviator James "Jimmy" Doolittle perform a solo aerobatic act and the Army team, the Three Musketeers, the event's centerpiece, put their three aircraft through formation and individual aerobatics. The Navy's representatives at the meet were not up to the same standards, having sent three fliers from three different squadrons, and Tomlinson was mortified. After a swig of liquid courage, he approached the Army team and finagled some of their secrets, including the use of a master jet in the carburetor, which provided for about half a minute of inverted flight. It is widely reported

that Tomlinson was taught how to fix a plane's carburetor for inverted flight by Jimmy Doolittle, although Tomlinson gave credit for the inverted fuel system to Al Williams.

The Spokane event made Tomlinson determined to see the Navy put together a top-notch demonstration team. Returning to his squadron, the Fighting Six of VB-2B, Tomlinson put his eagle eye on other squadron members as potential recruits. The two he chose were Bill Davis and Putt Storrs.

## Hard at Work

In January 1928, Fighting Six received new Boeing F2B-1 fighters replacing the old heavy, water-cooled FB5s. Practicing in semi-secrecy, Tomlinson was surprised to receive orders from Adm. Reeves to perform in San Francisco when the entire battle fleet was to gather and put on an airshow for the citizens of the Bay Area before steaming across the Pacific to the Hawaiian Islands.

A valuable public-relations source for the commanding officer of VB-2B, the Three Sea Hawks—though they had not yet selected that name—were a flashy bunch in the best Navy tradition. During the San Francisco show, the trio flipped over on their backs and flew inverted 2,000 feet over the Embarcadero. Sometimes, the team would fly as far as 2 miles while in the upside down position!

## You Have to Pick Your Moments

Sometimes it didn't really matter if the trio had an audience, although it could get a little dicey if the wrong person saw them doing the wrong thing at the wrong time. Such an event occured while they were in Hawaii, supposedly on training maneuvers. The trio were soon hard at it in a serious game of aerobatic one-upmanship against some upstart Army fliers. After a few loops and outside loops plus an inverted pass over the Army hangars for good measure, Tomlinson discovered that the commanding officer of the USS *Langley*, Capt. Jack Towers, had been on the sidelines watching the impromptu show.

Back aboard ship, the team awaited the worst. The captain informed the team that the "Army has been sufficiently impressed." Fortunately for the them, Towers said that he had failed to get the airplanes' numbers.

The trio were picked to lead the light bombing wing at the dedication of Lindbergh Field in San Diego, and led 30 aircraft in formation. Scheduled to make a mock strafing run over the reviewing stands, they did it from 5,000 feet above the clouds. The run was successful in Tomlinson's eyes—judging first from the Admiral being "tickled to pieces" as well as from the number of spectators who dove for the ground or ran.

## "Suicide Trio"

After performing their formation aerobatic act, the group was dubbed as the "Suicide Trio." Up to this point, they didn't have a name, and it now seemed an appropriate time to find one or be forever stuck with the unfortunate appellation given to them by the San Diego newspapers. It was team member Putt Storrs who came up with the name "Three Sea Hawks" and saved them from that terrible fate.

The Three Sea Hawks were selected to perform at the National Air Races at Mines Field (now referred to as Los Angeles International Airport) in September 1928. Part of their act included all three flying inverted down the show line and an incredible three consecutive loops at the end of a diving approach. Tomlinson claimed that not one of the loops was started more than 10 feet from the ground. Despite breaking all the rules for low-flying aerobatics—which Tomlinson learned from Earl Daugherty, now immortalized as Long Beach airport's Daugherty Field—Navy bigwigs congratulated the team.

## Tomlinson's Legacy

The Mines Field races were the last performance by the Three Sea Hawks; Tomlinson was soon detached from the Navy, but he had left a strong legacy. Attributing their success to "air discipline," Tomlinson described the Three Sea Hawks job as bringing the daily routine of a Navy pilot down to where the people could see it—much like the Blue Angels do today.

One thing that distinguishes the early military aerobatic teams from the sophisticated teams of today is that the early teams were basically doing this on a part-time basis, squeezing in practice when they could

or, in some cases, during "training maneuvers." They were not assigned this duty all the time, with support crews and the Navy's public-relations machine to support them. What they did with what they had is a remarkable testament to inventiveness, ingenuity, and inspiration.

## Other Navy Demonstration Teams

Other teams included the High Hatters of VF-1B and the Three T'Gallants'ls (pronounced "Three Gallant Souls"), formed in 1929 with instructors from VT-5 at Pensacola, Florida, (future home of the Blue Angels) and former Sea Hawk Lt. Bill Davis. Their maneuvers included the "Farvel"—a precursor to a maneuver the Blue Angels do today, the Double Farvel. The team began flying the Curtiss F6C-4, followed in 1930 by the Boeing F4B-1A and then the Boeing F2B-1.

The High Hatters, who flew from 1929 and into the early 1930s, were a nine-man squad that often flew roped together in sections of three from takeoff, through a loop to a landing—even taxiing in while strapped together. Notably, three of the High Hatters went on to achieve flag rank: Lt. L.E. Gehres, Lt. (j.g.) F. N. Kivette, and Lt. (j.g.) F. O'Beirne. One of the team's highlights was flying with Col. Charles Lindbergh during the National Air Races in 1929.

Another new team, the Three Flying Fish, leapt into the air in 1930 in Curtiss F6C-4s at the direction of Adm. Moffett. Admiral Moffett put one of the Navy's best aerobatic pilots, Lt. Al Williams, in charge. But, after Williams left the team, M. B. Gardner inherited the team—and Williams' aerobatically modified aircraft. The team's unusual name was drummed up in a contest run by war correspondent Ernie Pyle (many wags claim it was Pyle's girlfriend who picked the name). Helping to provide some continuity, Putt Storrs (formerly of the Three Sea Hawks) was a member of this team as well. This short-lived team was disbanded on April 15, 1931, but it also spawned successful careers for its participants, such as a young Lt. Frederick Trapnell who, in 1943, became the first Navy pilot to fly a jet (the Bell Airacomet) and M. B. Gardner, who became commanding officer of the carrier USS *Enterprise* during World War II in the Pacific.

Also in 1930, the US Marine Corps formed its own team from VF-9M, based at Quantico, Virginia. By the mid-1930s, the Marines were flying an amazing 18 Curtiss F4B-4s, doing loops, wingovers, squirrel-cage maneuvers (two groups flying loops), and dive-bombing in three-plane sections.

Unfortunately, just as things were beginning to get interesting, World War II to intervened, and all pilots, planes, and aviation fuel were directed to the war effort. There would be no more of the popular exhibitions until the Blue Angels took to the skies in 1946.

## Birth of the Blues

By the spring of 1946, thousands of veterans had returned to the States to rebuild their lives. America's military was down-sizing. Thousands of surplus aircraft and vehicles sat in storage yards across the country. The country was trying to pick up the pieces after being embroiled in four years of World War.

While the nation demobilized, it was business as usual for the armed forces, albeit on a much smaller scale. During World War II, an awesome weapon came into its own—the aircraft carrier. Although down-sizing, the Navy needed men to sail these floating air bases. A new breed of warrior would also need to be trained to operate off these floating runways—the Naval Aviator.

Something was needed to encourage young men to join the Navy and consider Naval Aviation as a career. The question was how to get the Navy's message to such land-locked areas as Omaha, Nebraska; Denver, Colorado; and Boise, Idaho? The Navy needed a vehicle to promote the romance of flight and the mystique and pride of becoming a Naval Aviator.

A flight exhibition team would be the answer. They could show off the skills of the Navy's most experienced pilots, display front-line aircraft, talk to young men about a career in the Navy, and they could positively portray the image of the US Navy away from the coasts.

The energy to launch a Naval flight demonstration team started in the Secretary of the Navy's public affairs division. Capt. Roy Sempler, in the public affairs division's office of the chief of information, was the driving force. A dispatch came down from the Secretary of the Navy through the Chief of Naval Operations down to the chief of Naval Air Training, VAdm. Frank Wagner at Pensacola. The dispatch said (paraphrased), "Request your thinking on the advisability of establishing a flying unit to represent Naval Aviation and the Navy in whole to the young military aviators, but also when directed, to appear at public events (airshows, etc.); request your comments, earliest. . ."

When this dispatch reached RAdm. Ralph Davidson, chief of Naval Air Advanced Training Command, he handed it down to Cdr. Hugh Winters who asked LCdr. Roy M. "Butch" Voris to put some thoughts down on paper about forming a flying team.

Hellcats of the Navy's Flight Exhibition Team on the tarmac at the Craig Field dedication, June 15, 1946. Craig Field was the site of the team's first public performance. *Voris collection*

Voris had received his ensign's commission at NAS Corpus Christi, Texas, in February 1942. He then flew Grumman F4F Wildcats with VF-10, The Grim Reapers, from the USS *Enterprise* and from Guadalcanal where he was shot down. For his second combat tour, he flew Grumman F6F Hellcats with VF-2 aboard the USS *Hornet*. During his tour on board the USS *Hornet*, Voris was chosen by Cdr. E. H. "Butch" O'Hare to fly experimental night-fighter operations at Tarawa. His record included seven confirmed aerial victories, three probables, three Distinguished Flying Crosses, 11 Air Medals, and the Purple Heart, among other decorations. After the war he was chief flight officer of the Instructors Advanced Training Unit (IATU) and was responsible for training officers for the Advanced Training Command. Voris was well-rounded and respected, a result of his combat experience and flying ability, as well as his administration and command experience. He was an excellent choice to provide a feasibility paper on a flight-demonstration team.

Voris' written answer went back up through channels to Washington. They replied, "Concur in advisability of establishing such a team." Then a dispatch officially came back down from Washington, and it said, "Proceed earliest." That was April 24, 1946.

Voris was selected as officer in charge and given the task of forming and training a team at NAS Jacksonville, Florida. His goal was to have the team ready to fly by June 15, 1946. He recalled the process of starting up the team:

> When I was given the job to form the team, there were no instructions. Nobody had any, and nobody tried to give me any. The staff told me to draw up a list of what I wanted in terms of aircraft and people, and they would get them for me. It was formed in the training command. There was two reasons for this. Number one, it was in what would nowadays be called a "draw-down." It was after the war, and they were cutting forces, people, material, and so forth. And here the Navy was going to spend money on building a stunt team? In the training command they could keep us away from public view, out over the swamps. "Fly for

The team taxies out past the crowd at Craig Field. The show at Craig Field was dubbed the Southeastern Air Show and Exhibition. The team's pilots showcased the abilities of those in the Navy's Advanced Training Command. *Voris collection*

the Alligators or whatever's out there," they said. The second reason for basing the team with the training command was support for the F6Fs. The Advanced Training Command was already flying the type. Plus, the team was to provide the incentive and the morale for young pilots coming along and eventually to interest youngsters not yet in aviation to make Naval Aviation their career choice.

Cdr. Hugh Winters was the officer in charge of the IATU. Voris was responsible to Winters, who then reported to the chief of Naval Air Advanced Training. Winters' command provided materials support and records administration. Because the team was not a command, Voris became the officer in charge of what would be known as the Navy Flight Exhibition Team.

## Putting the Wheels in Motion

Voris continued:

I set the team up as all bachelors. I was a bachelor, so everybody's going to be a bachelor. We were not going to worry about children at this stage of the game.

I was familiar with the "Hose Nose" [F4U Corsair] and the FM-2, which was the General Motors-built Grumman F4F Wildcat; the only one I did not want to play with was the Grumman F7F Tigercat. It was just too big and it would take a lot more maintenance support.

I started getting the FGF Hellcats ordered in, getting the pilots selected, and getting the crew.

Voris hand-picked the crew that would maintain the team's aircraft. Each man was regarded as being the best in his rate. Standing, from left: unidentified, Voris, plane captain L. R. Reed, unidentified; kneeling, R. M. Borndeaux. *Voris collection*

Voris selected 11 men for the ground crew, each the best in his rate: C. W. Barber, R. M. Borndeaux, C. H. Casey, H. B. Hardee, C. C. Hicks, L. J. Johnson, W. L. Miller, L. R. Reid, W. E. Stanzeski, J. D. Turrentine, and T. P. Valentiner. Three Grumman technical representatives were also on hand to help overcome any aircraft-related problems. They were Bill Babington, Fred Benson, and "Goldie" Glenn.

The flight officers selected to serve on the team were LCdr. L. G. Barnard, Lt. (j.g.) M. W. "Mel" Cassidy, and Lt. M. N. "Wick" Wickendoll. Barnard was assigned to another command, and Lt. (j.g.) Gale Stouse replaced him. Stouse would fly the SNJ single-engine, tandem-seat trainer as the Japanese Zero in the act.

The Hellcats came from overhaul and repair. They had gone through an operational cycle and had then been rebuilt. The team did some minor modifications to the planes to lighten them as much as possible. The guns, ammo boxes, oil-tank armor, and a number of smaller items were removed. Once these items were out, they had to sweat 50 pounds of lead on the tailhook to keep the center of gravity within its fore and aft limits. During shows, the team flew with only one of the three gas tanks, the internal fuselage centerline tank, partially full of fuel.

The colors of the airplanes, blue and gold, are the Navy's colors. Said Voris:

> They are not as splashy as the Thunderbirds with the red, white, and blue, but I picked the colors. Insignia blue, it's a lighter blue than the normal fleet airplane blue. It has a deeper luster and is accented with the gold or yellow paint. All of the markings were painted in the yellow—the "US Navy" on the side and "Navy" under the wings, with the large numbers on the tail.
>
> I got a letter recently from my painter. I had a painter in the organization to clean up nicks and dents. He said, "Boss, I don't know how you did it and got all that gold leaf, but our first airplanes were in gold leaf in 1946." I looked back on it and I'd forgotten all about that. They had actually gotten gold leaf to put on the airplanes. Everything that was gold was gold leaf—US Navy under the wings and on both sides of the fuselage, the tail number, and the Bureau number. Somehow, somewhere within the Navy, somebody said we are going to do it right. I didn't ask for it. I didn't even know what gold leaf was really. Our paint job was very beautiful, and it has followed through over the years. The shade of blue changes a little bit now and then, but it has followed through; the markings are almost the same as they were the first day.

## Agendas and Objectives

The Secretary of the Navy's office had a separate agenda in forming the team. Their bottom-line objective was to garner a larger share of the defense appropriations funds for the Navy and Naval Aviation, specifically funds to build aircraft carriers. "In peacetime back then," Voris said, "you did not see much about Naval Aviation and the carriers. We needed to show off Naval Aviation and remind the spectators what the carrier pilots did."

The subordinate objective was the motivation of young Naval Aviators—giving them an objective toward which to aspire. But Voris had his own objectives:

> That's beat Army; then it was the Army Air Forces. . . . I figured that if I could do that, then all the other stuff would fall in the basket. Now, since that's my motivation, what am I going to do in the air that's going to be better than Army aviation can do, will do, or commit to do? I said, OK, we are going to have to put a little risk into this thing. As much risk as the system can safely tolerate—because if you misjudge that, then the game's over with.
>
> I started with three airplanes as the base unit. It later was changed to reduce the risk and because we were using a tactical unit of four—two elements of two. All of our rolls, with the exception of one or two maneuvers, are going to be rolls in position on the axis of each individual airplane. This translates into being blind half-way around the roll—either the first half or the second half of the roll. This should give them [Army] something to jump at.

"I wanted the maneuvers fast. I wanted the show tight. And I wanted to get it down and not stooge around repeating a maneuver. I never repeated a maneuver in a show, 17 minutes from on the show line to off the show line at the end. It was fast. In my mind it was, "Get it up, get it on, get it down." That was the concept I had, and that's what we followed in building the team.

The first flight of the Navy's Flight Exhibition Team was on May 10, 1946.

## Getting the Go-Ahead

Voris and the team had been practicing for a while, and it did not look like they were going to get into any trouble. Cmdr. Dan Smith, director of training for the Naval Air Advanced Training Command, wanted to take a look at Voris' progress to determine whether the team was ready to perform or should be disbanded. Smith asked Voris and the team to meet him at an outlying airstrip near Cecil Field, Florida. Smith flew in an F6F and kept it running while Voris brought the team over and flew the show. Voris was not going to land, and Smith radioed that he would meet the team back at NAS Jacksonville. "I went ahead and did a little more practicing, Voris said, "and he was at the field when we landed. The first thing he said to me was 'You crazy sons of bitches. You're going to kill yourselves.' I said, 'No, no, no.' He said he liked it, and that he would recommend that the admiral see it."

Two days later, at about five o'clock in the evening, the Navy's Flight Demonstration Team flew over to the main site at NAS Jacksonville to fly their routine for RAdm. Ralph Davidson. Voris said, "It went perfectly." Adm. Davidson then recommended that his boss, VAdm. Frank Wagner, see the team perform. Wagner would advise the Secretary of the Navy whether the team was ready or not. Voris led the team back to NAS Jacksonville to perform for the admiral. He remembered:

> It was a nice day. The admiral was there and about four or five captains, horse-holders, and so forth. We got to the point of the combat segment of the show. The brass was sitting there in a set of folding chairs out on the parking ramp, pretty close to the flight line.
>
> Here we come. We shoot down the Zero and out goes the dummy pilot. The static cord fails, and the parachute does not open. The dummy full of sand and sawdust, chute still packed, hits about 5 feet in front of the admiral's group. It could have killed half of them if it had hit them. It just exploded, sand and sawdust flew everywhere. So we went ahead and did the rest of the

The NAS Jacksonville base newspaper hailed the first performance of the Flight Exhibition Team. *Voris collection*

show. Nobody said anything, but I saw what had happened. We finished the show and landed, pulled up, and got out. I walked over to the admiral's party, and they were still sitting down and talking to each other. I knelt down on one knee in front of them because they were still seated, and the admiral was shaking his head. About that time, I thought I was looking at a court-martial, and he said, "Voris, I've got one suggestion: Move it out a little further on the field just in case that happens again."

Adm. Wagner liked it and informed the Secretary of the Navy that the team was ready to perform. "That's how it all got started," Voris said.

The team was ready to perform. The June 15, 1946, Southeastern Air Show and Exhibition at Craig Field, Jacksonville, Florida, was their first show. Lt. Alfred "Al" Taddeo joined the team right after their performance at Craig Field. They then went on and flew at Nimitz Day, NAS Corpus Christi, Texas; Des Moines, Iowa; Kansas City, Missouri; Pensacola, Florida; and Omaha, Nebraska.

## Flying The Airshow
The Hellcat had an R-2800-30W and it could put out about 1,800 horsepower, but the team could not pull all of that power because they had to have flexibility for the wingman. To open the show, they would run in to build speed (in a three-plane vee) down over the runway and then up into a loop. Voris described the act:

Out of the loop into a full Cuban Eight. Out of that into a chandelle turn. Out of that into a vee roll—that's where you rolled the whole formation around the formation's axis. Things were done low, maybe 50 feet on the entry and 75 feet on the exit. We could do it because nobody was telling us not to. (The FAA became more intimate with us later on . . .) From that we went into a Reverse Echelon Roll—we took the echelon in the vee, rolled it upside down, and changed positions in the roll. Then out of that into a roll to the left in left echelon—where the whole formation is rolling left [around the leader's axis]. Out of that, we went into a chandelle turn off the field, climbing for altitude.

We had an SNJ trainer that was painted up as a Japanese Zero—yellow with a great big meatball on it, with smoke canisters, and dummy .30-calibers pointing through the propeller, and the rear-seat man, the plane captain, had a dummy pilot in a flight suit with a parachute that he held on his lap. The war was just over, really, and combat things were still on people's minds. The SNJ would come in over the stands, do a chandelle turn, and the crowd would wonder what it was because the SNJ's appearance was unexpected. We [the formation] would be in position to start our first run [simulated gunnery attacks] on the SNJ. We would mix it up for maybe 3 minutes and he would fire his .30-caliber for a little noise. After a couple of runs, he would fire a smoke canister. He would be streaming smoke and acting like he's wounded. Then he would pull up into a turn, and at low negative-g, out would pop the dummy pilot and parachute. It would float down, and the crash crews would race out. It was kind of "Hokus Pokus." Everybody thought he was really shot down. There was screaming in the stands, and as the crash crew went out, we were climbing for the last part of the show.

We came in, entered with a reverse Half Cuban Eight and echeloned up, rolling on in, back down and through—we were rolling on each aircraft's own axis, but in formation. You've got to have a lot of confidence in everybody. Then back down across, followed by inverted flight. The length of an inverted pass was limited by fuel pressure in the Bearcat, and oil pressure in the Hellcat. We would roll inverted in a vee again—around our own individual axis. We were low, maybe 100 feet. It took a lot of stick force keeping it up. Then across the field inverted; then we rolled out and closed the show. We were able to hold specifically to this routine for each show.

After landing, the pilots would taxi up to the line, then walk the line and sign autographs. "We would pat the little kiddies on the head, and shake hands with the moms and dads," Voris said. "That was essentially it—get it up, get it on, get it down."

## How the Blues Got Their Name
Let's face it, "The Flight Exhibition Team" is not a very catchy name. To find a new name,

the team ran a contest throughout the training command, and Voris described how the winner was picked:

> We were getting hundreds of names back, but not a one grabbed us like we wanted to be grabbed. I got a call to go up to the staff, this time to meet with the chief of staff, Capt. Bill Gentner. He asked how the name contest was coming. I told him that we were just not finding anything right yet, but that I was sure we would get something soon. Gentner told me he had one for me to consider, the Navy's "Blue Lancers." Something rung a bell: I remembered that his son had submitted this one. I said, "Yeah, its got a ring to it, hasn't it, Captain." He asked me to give it serious thought, and I knew what he meant.
>
> We were going to go to New York for a show, and Wickendoll, who was my No. 2 man, was looking through the *New Yorker* magazine. We were sitting having a scotch in my room at the BOQ [bachelor officers quarters], and he said, "I've got it, Boss." I asked what he meant. He was looking at a column called Goings On About Town, and the nightclubs were all listed. The Blue Angel nightclub was a big thing in its day. I think it took up a whole block. Four orchestras, eight or nine bars—it was massive. I said, "Gee, that sounds great! The Blue Angels. Navy, blue, and flying!"

When they arrived at Omaha, Nebraska, for the airshow, they told the aviation press of their Blue Lancers versus Blue Angels dilemma. The press agreed to help. After the show, headlines touted the team's performance with the name Blue Angels in quotes, Voris continued:

> When I got back to Jacksonville with the team, I was summoned up to Gentner's office. Dispatches had come in congratulating the command on the performance of the team. He asked, "What's this Blue Angel stuff?" I told him I did not know and that I had heard some comment, from somebody in the press, saying they are just like Blue Angels.

First show, first trophy. The team was awarded this trophy for most outstanding aerial performance at the June 15, 1946, Southeastern Air Show and Exhibition. Voris displays the trophy to Capt. William E. Gentner, Jr. The team had transitioned into the Bearcat when this photo was taken. This trophy was recently refurbished and is now at the Blue Angels' home base at Pensacola, Florida. *Voris collection*

Capt. Gentner knew he had been hoodwinked, but there was nothing he could do.

## Settling in for the Season

The ranks of the Blue Angels had doubled since the first airshow. Voris, Wickendoll (on right wing), Taddeo (on left wing), and Stouse (in the SNJ/Zero) had been joined by Lt. (j.g.) Ross "Robby" Robinson (reliever SNJ/Zero pilot) and Lt. William "Billy" May (spare pilot).

The team flew Hellcats at Jacksonville, Corpus Christi, Des Moines, Kansas City, Pensacola, Omaha, and at Mayport, Florida. Then, word came down that the team was going to be assigned Grumman F8F Bearcats.

The Hellcats flew their final show at Grumman's Bethpage, New York, factory.

The Blue Angels at Grumman's Bethpage factory accepting
a factory-fresh F8F-1. From left: May, Wickendoll, Voris, Knight.
*Voris collection*

# Chapter Two

# Bearcats to Panther Jets

When the Blue Angels received approval to transition to the Bearcat, Grumman agreed to modify the aircraft, strip them, paint them, and do all of the conversion work at the Bethpage factory. The Blue Angels flew up to Grumman for a farewell show in the F6F Hellcats on August 15, 1946. Voris described the show:

Rare color photo shot in late 1949 or early 1950 of the team's F9F-2s with their wings folded. *John M. Campbell collection*

> They turned all the Grummanites out that day. Workers were lined up on both sides of the runway, and we did a show. We landed, got out of the airplanes, and turned them over to the Navy's Bureau of Aeronautics representative and picked up our new Bearcats.
>
> We each had one flight in an airplane that was being readied for delivery to the fleet. Our particular airplanes had not been test-flown. They were just coming out of the barn with new paint jobs. I insisted on taking the planes around the field a couple of times to make sure that they were not throwing oil and that there was nothing else wrong. Everything seemed to shape up pretty good, so we headed out to our first stop, Navy Norfolk, Virginia.

## Headed for Trouble

The flight to Norfolk turned out to be eventful, as Voris recalled:

> We were going to pick up fuel at Norfolk, and I wanted to see somebody there. We were coasting down the Atlantic coast to Norfolk, and I called the tower 15 to 20 miles out for landing. Four Bearcats. I was given clearance to land, and I broke the flight, so we would be making individual landings. We had landed the airplane only once. I'm rolling the trim back as I'm slowing down and slowing down, and my trim wheel is hitting metal. I'm having to

Bearcat No. 5 at Bethpage. Note the yellow SNJ that doubled as a Japanese Zero during the airshow. *Grumman via Voris collection*

pull the stick all the way back to keep the nose up. Something is drastically wrong. I don't know what it is—if it's in the controls, center of gravity, or what. I told Navy Norfolk tower that I was pulling up out of the landing circle because I had a problem.

Then the tower came back, "Grumman Corp. advises aircraft unsafe for flight; you are grounded." They are telling me this while I'm in the air! By that time my wheels are all working and "Wick," my No. 2 man, came on the radio and reported that he had the same problem. While this was going on, Nos. 3 and 4 reported the same problem. I instructed everybody to pull out of the landing pattern and to keep their speed up. I remembered the last thing I talked about with the chief engineer before getting in that airplane at Grumman. I asked him how come he did not have to sweat any lead around the tail hook to keep the CG [center of gravity] within limits?

He said, "We've been through that, Butch. You're lucky, we don't have to do that, so you get rid of that weight." I thanked him and did not think anything more of it until arriving at Norfolk.

After we took off, Grumman's chief engineer went back to the drawing boards in engineering, and they reviewed the numbers again. They confirmed the danger, our CG had traveled forward as we burned the fuel down.

I pulled out to the side, by myself, and slowed the plane down. If I put flaps down it pitched over further. What I was able to do, was to figure out that with about an inch left before the stick hit the aft stop I could slow to about 135–140 knots. That's hot, but it was either land at that speed or bail out and loose all these beautiful airplanes. So I went ahead and wheeled it on and got it stopped. I radioed to the others, "Leave your flaps up, leave yourself full back tab, and then if you add power the nose will come up." We all got down, saving the airplanes. I went in and was on the phone with Grumman-Bethpage and the Grumman representative was there. We had to get back because we had the Cleveland National Air Races staring us in the face with this new Bearcat. We now had a total of 1 hour and 20 or 30 minutes in the airplane. We had a lot of work to do. I asked Grumman if I could get the aircraft home to Jacksonville anyway semi-safe? They worked on it and told me that if we did not burn down below a certain point on fuel, and if we stopped every couple hundred miles to refill our tanks, we could get there. This was with the understanding that we were going to have to carry more speed. I Ok'd it, and we hopped all the way back to Jacksonville, where we immediately put the planes into overhaul and repair and on went 50 pounds of sheet lead. We took the hook out and sweated the lead sheet on it and then bolted the hook back in.

The team started training immediately because the National Air Races were rapidly approaching. "The airplane was magnificent," said Voris. "We used the same maneuvers. The Bearcat just gave us more power, and we could go a little higher and a little faster."

The team flew one show at Hutcheson, Kansas, before leaving for the nationals. They flew via Denver to the dedication of Stapleton International Airport and flew a great show. "We then proceeded to Cleveland," said Voris, "refueling at Omaha, but we had problems with the airplanes. . . . Some were working and some were not. We finally made Cleveland and the races, and did a real good job there."

By the time the Blue Angels arrived in Cleveland, they were receiving a tremendous amount of media attention—especially in the aviation press. The National Air Races were as big an event then as the Superbowl is today. The four-day event would be front-page news around the country. "There wasn't anything bigger than the National Air Races at Cleveland," Voris said. "All the big players were there. We did real well. The team showed off real well. That's where we really came into our own right and were recognized. From then on we got more and more requests to perform all over the country."

## The Loss of the First Blue Angel

The Bearcat was a light airplane with 2,400 horsepower when using alcohol-water augmentation. The outer 32 inches of the wing panel was unique. Instead of the full row of rivets, Grumman engineers left out every other rivet so it would break off if you overstressed the airplane. Rather than failing at the wing root, the outer wing panel would fail, thereby reducing the air load on the wing, thus saving the pilot. Unfortunately, they almost never came off together. Many times, one panel would come off, producing asymmetrical lift, sending the airplane into a death spiral.

The next version of the wing panels used explosive tips with a thermite cord cross-connected so that both panels would blow off at the same time. Many times those would go off when the aircraft was just sitting out on the parking ramp.

Spare pilot Lt. "Robby" Robinson was lost at the show in Jacksonville, Florida, four shows before the end of the season on September 29, 1946. This was the Blue Angels' first show at home in the F8Fs. Voris described that fateful day:

Over 6 feet tall, Voris would wear out the shoulders of his flying suits in the narrow cockpit. *Voris collection*

Beautiful study of "Butch" Voris' No. 1 F8F Bearcat at NRAB Oakland, California, prior to the team's October 9, 1946, performance. *William T. Larkins*

We had pretty lousy weather. It was just haze; you couldn't see. Robinson hesitated in a Cuban Eight with a double roll, between the first and second roll. He hesitated just long enough to where he had to over-pull, over-stressing the wings, and he snapped the wing tip off. Only one panel separated, causing asymmetrical lift, and he rolled into the ground. It was a bleak day for the team.

## Leaving the First Team

During the Denver show, on the way to the National Air Races, LCdr. Bob Clarke flew in from Patuxent River, Maryland, with a Ryan Fireball, and Voris was immediately impressed, as he recalled:

He flew in the show schedule, and that's where I got to know him. He went on to Cleveland with us to perform there, and then I saw him a few more times. I knew he was an outstanding pilot. One day, I asked him if he would be interested in relieving me. He said it would be a real honor. It was being left up to me to pick my successor, so I got him ordered into the team to relieve me. Before I left, he rode double for quite a while. He also practiced by himself, learning, just doing what he could.

I started looking at who would succeed Clarke because I felt I had a personal stake in this thing. Clarke and I went up to Patuxent River, where the operations officer was LCdr. Dusty Rhodes, who had been in Fighting 10 on board *Enterprise* with me early in the war. Rhodes had been shot down, and he was picked up by a Japanese submarine during the Battle of Santa Cruz. He was interned in Yokohama Prison Camp No. 1, then transferred to No. 2, where he spent the rest of the war. I thought this would be a good opportunity to get him back into the swing of things. I didn't tell Rhodes why I was coming to see him, or that I was bringing Bob Clarke with me. I remember his eyes when we approached him. They got bigger, and bigger, and bigger. He was excited about joining the Blue Angels. That's how the third leader came about.

## Building on a Solid Foundation

LCdr. R. A. "Bob" Clarke relieved Cmdr. Voris on May 30, 1947. Clarke continued the three-plane vee formation and began to practice what has become known as the four-plane "Diamond." Two new maneuvers were introduced at the 1947 National Championship Air Races in Cleveland, Ohio: the Diamond Loop and the Diamond Barrel Roll. The four-Bearcat formation also split into two two-plane elements to pursue the SNJ/Zero. This gunnery maneuver, the "Thatch Weave," was a crowd-pleaser.

Voris' influence did indeed carry over to the third Blue Angels commanding officer when LCdr. R.E. "Dusty" Rhodes assumed command of the squadron on January 9, 1948.

World War II was slowly fading in the distance, and the SNJ/Zero had its fuselage "meatballs" removed and the markings "US Navy" added in their place. The SNJ had also been nicknamed *Beetle Bomb* by members of the team. The SNJ was getting old, and it was incompatible, speed-wise, with the F8Fs. Its days were clearly numbered.

New maneuvers introduced included the Reverse Echelon Roll and a Cuban Eight flown in Finger Tip formation.

When Naval Air Advanced Training moved to Corpus Christi in fall 1948, the team moved with them.

The team acquired the full-time use of an R4D to support its movements in the 1949 season. This would be the first in a changing series of support aircraft until the C-130 joined the team in 1970.

Lt. J. H. "Jake" Robcke joined the team for the 1949 show season, already up to speed in the F8F, as he recalled:

Lt. Al Taddeo's F8F-1 at Oakland after the airshow. *William T. Larkins*

Cmdr. Voris is greeted upon his arrival at NRAB Oakland by commanding officer Capt. Baker. *William T. Larkins*

I reported in, and it just so happens that I was flying F8F Bearcats (with VF-11) and the team was flying Bearcats. At the time, the rule was that all the pilots were supposed to be combat experienced, single, and preferably checked out in the aircraft that the team was flying. I think I was the first pilot that ever reported in with any time in the Bearcat.

His first airshow as a Blue Angel was at the All American Air Maneuvers in Miami, Florida, held January 7–9, 1949. Robcke was the SNJ *Beetle Bomb*'s pilot. He described his job:

*Beetle Bomb* was a clay pigeon. We were a target. *Beetle Bomb* had a big "0" painted on it, which was supposed to designate an enemy air-

craft. The show would start with the F8Fs doing a pretty phenomenal thing, at least to me; they would take off, fold their gear up, get to the end of the runway, and then go right over the top in a Half Cuban Eight. Then, they would form up and do the Diamond routine. As they did their last Diamond Roll, *Beetle Bomb*'s job was to come roaring in to the runway, behind and underneath the formation, and then do a Half Cuban Eight off the deck. In the meantime, the F8Fs would split into two two-plane sections and bracket the SNJ as it came back down the line. The F8Fs would make coordinated simulated gunnery passes. The SNJ was equipped with three or four smoke grenades under the belly, and after the first pass, I would trip one. The airplane would

The Blue Angels at Oakland. From left: unidentified, public-information officer Barney Barnetts, Voris, unidentified, unidentified, Wickendoll, May, unidentified. *William T. Larkins*

start smoking, simulating a hit. Then my job was to flop around and somehow do a 180-degree turn and come back down the runway. The F8Fs would maintain their bracket and make another coordinated simulated gunnery run. This time the plane was really hurt. I had to simulate that the airplane was really out of control. The guy in the back seat had a dummy with a parachute and it was my job to hang up low and slow in a steep turn, and he would throw the dummy out. Then I had to simulate that the airplane was completely out of control, no pilot, and try to find something to hide behind, simulating a crash.

At Elmira, New York, the kid in the back seat put the dummy up on the edge of the cockpit, and the slipstream snatched it out of

his hands before he was ready to let it go. I had not gotten up into the proper position, so the dummy went back, hit the rudder, and jammed it over some. Fortunately, it jammed it with right rudder. When I felt the jolt, my first inclination was to make sure I had plenty of airspeed and control of the airplane. The faster I went, the less control I had. I was headed in about the proper direction for landing, so I slow-flight tested it and made a completely normal landing.

After flying *Beetle Bomb*, Robcke moved into the Bearcat Diamond as slot pilot.

Shortly after the Elmira incident, the SNJ was retired in favor of an F8F *Beetle Bomb*. A centerline pod was rigged to the F8F to hold

SNJ-6 BuNo. 112193 before the show at Oakland, October 9, 1946. Note the "meatball" on the fuselage. The war had ended only one year before, and the team's demonstration of aerial gunnery techniques was a crowd-pleaser. *William T. Larkins*

the parachute-rigged dummy. The smoke canisters were fitted into the tailhook well, and the show continued with the same routine. After the Blue Angels transitioned to jets, the F8F *Beetle Bomb*'s speed differential was found to be incompatible. *Beetle Bomb* was turned over to the "Blab" to be used as an advance airplane. "We referred to the announcer as the 'Blab,'" said Robcke, "because, originally, and I think they are back to it now, the newest pilot to join the team would be the 'Blab.' Later, we got a person whose only job was public relations, and he did the announcing."

The jet era was coming to the Blues. It would have its fits and starts, but the days of propeller-driven air-superiority fighters were over. Robcke reflected on the team's use of the Bearcat:

It was a fun airplane to fly. We could not fly nearly as close with that big fan up front, but you could do some things you could never do later in the jets, such as the Half Cuban Eight on takeoff. The F8Fs had so much power and accel-

erated so rapidly that you had plenty of speed to go over the top by the end of the runway. It got kind of dicey at places like Denver [because of density altitude], but it was a fantastic airplane. The F8F was fairly short-legged. It only carried 185 gallons of fuel internally. Cranked back like that engine could be in that airplane, you could get below 50 gallons per hour, just cruising. But that's not the way we flew with Dusty up front. He was always in a hurry. We had to cruise at 235 knots, so we landed fairly frequently.

We had a relatively small maintenance crew, and they were all extremely dedicated. Good troops every one of them. I don't remember ever having a bird down for a show—unlike the problems we had with the F9Fs when they were brand new.

## Enter the Panther Jets

The team went through jet training at San Diego with VF-52 in June 1949. At that time, Air Group 5 had not been to sea for a while, and they were used as a guinea-pig air group. The Navy

The team met the St. Louis Cardinals at their winter training ground at St. Petersberg, Florida. Blue Angels from left to right: Voris, Wickendoll, May. *Voris collection*

took one of Air Group 5's squadrons, VF-52, and equipped them with Air Force F-80Cs, which the Navy designated TO-1. Robcke's first flight in a TO-1 was June 11, 1949. The transition training course lasted 10.9 hours.

"We flew one show at Olathe, Kansas, [in F8Fs] and then flew to Bethpage to pick up the F9F-2s," said Robcke. "My first flight in an F9F-2 was on July 14, 1949. [LCdr.] Ray Hawkins and I volunteered to stay at Bethpage to wait for the first couple of planes to be ready. Then we ferried them down to Corpus Christi."

Although they had taken delivery of the first jets, the team continued to fly the F8Fs during airshow performances. Robcke told why:

> We faced a specific problem with the F9Fs. Being the first aircraft of their type in the training

Part of the team's duties included personal appearances at public functions. The team attended the crowning of Miss Universe at Long Beach, California. Cdr. Voris presents the trophy to Miss Congeniality. *Voris collection*

The Diamond pilots prepare to take off in formation. Shortly after this photo was taken, the team transitioned into the F9F-2 Panther. *John M. Campbell collection*

command, and being a brand new airplane, we did not have the support equipment we needed. We had to build our own starting unit for these engines. The F9F-2 had a Pratt & Whitney license-built Rolls Royce Nene engine in it—a good engine, extremely reliable. There were some glitches. The original starters were not all that reliable. One of the first shows we flew was a two-plane show because the starters broke in all the other airplanes. The F9F required a totally different starter than the Air Force F-80s and Navy TOs. It was called a constant-current start. We had the overhaul and repair shop at Corpus Christi build us this great big wagon with all kinds of batteries with buss bars. This allowed us to start up with a very low load and just keep increasing it until you got the engine wound up. You had to have the engine turning about 10 percent in order to start.

The first airshow flown in the F9F-2 was on August 20, 1949 at Beaumont, Texas. It was quickly evident that the show could not be kept

as close to the audience as it was with the propeller-driven Bearcats. In the Panthers, high speed maneuvers required the formation to be quite a distance from the field.

## The Rope Trick

The team continued to work on new routines to go with their new jets. Robcke recalled:

> When we flew at the National Air Races [September 4 and 5], we might have averaged about 25 hours total jet time and maybe 15 hours in type. We were trying to come up with something unusual, so somebody thought about tying the first three airplanes together. The idea was to tie a cord from the inboard wings of both wingman, and then the boss would pop his speed brakes, which are on the bottom of the fuselage, and then shove the ends of the bungee cords into his speed brakes when he cranked them closed. That way we took off tied together and when we were through with the Diamond routine, the boss

would pop his speed brakes and the bungee cords would come loose.

We flew an entire practice airshow at Corpus Christi tied together, and it worked beautifully. We took off at Cleveland with the first three tied together and the bungee cords broke before we got to do the actual show.

That was the end of the "Rope Trick."

The team transferred home fields fairly early in the jet era, shortly after the appearance at Cleveland. They were sharing the field with patrol-bomber squadrons and were incompatible. The Navy had taken VF-52 and designated it as JTU-1 (Jet Training Unit One) and transferred it to Whiting Field near Pensacola. "When that was established," Robcke said, "there were all these jets operating out of north field at Whiting." On September 10, 1949, the Blue Angels transferred from Corpus Christi to Whiting Field. Less than a month later, on November 2, 7, and 8, the team flew for *Life* magazine photographers. The photos and a story on the Blue Angels was published in the November 28, 1949, edition. This copy of the magazine is now a collector's item.

## Magda Takes Over; Korean War Shorten's Show Season

LCdr. Johnny Magda relieved Rhodes as officer in charge on January 11, 1950. When Magda had arrived and was training under Rhodes, he suggested that he fill in during the lull when the Diamond was out of view. He got authorization to do so, and a single solo position was created on the team.

The team flew their first show in the new Grumman F9F-2 on August 20, 1949, at Beaumont, Texas. Here, F9F-2 BuNo. 123016 sits at the National Air Races, September 4–5, 1949, at Cleveland, Ohio. Prior to the team's performance at the races, they had successfully flown with the three Diamond aircraft "roped" together. Unfortunately, at the races, one of the ropes broke in the air prior to the show, and the maneuver was dropped. *William T. Larkins collection*

Once the team acquired jets, an aircraft with compatible speeds was needed to replace the SNJ *Beetle Bomb*. F8F-1 BuNo. 95187 replaced the SNJ in the *Beetle Bomb* role. The canister between the landing-gear doors would eject a rather compact dummy pilot and parachute to simulate being shot down. This aircraft was destroyed April 24, 1950, when Bob Longworth attempted to execute a roll on takeoff. Longworth's death ended the *Beetle Bomb* routine. *John M. Campbell collection*

On April 24, Lt. Bob Longworth perished in the F8F *Beetle Bomb*. Tragedy had struck the team again. Robcke recalled the fatal incident:

> We were scheduled to fly an airshow over the training carrier at Pensacola. All I know is that his plane captain told me that Longworth was going to do a roll on takeoff. And he almost did, but not quite.

Longworth's unfortunate death was also the end of *Beetle Bomb*. But the new jets continued to impress, as Robcke recalled:

> After the show at Niagara Falls, on June 26, on the way home, [Lt.] Pat Murphy had a problem, and he had to go into Columbus, Ohio. His aircraft was down for a part. I flew from the Canadian border to the Gulf of Mexico in 2.3 hours, found out what kind of part Murphy needed, and that same afternoon I leaped back into my bird and got to Columbus, Ohio, in 2 hours to deliver the part. Four point three hours total that day from Niagara Falls to the Pensacola area and back to Columbus, Ohio. It kind of impressed me.

It was decided up at the Chief of Naval Operations level that since there was a war on, it would make good public relations for the Navy to send these guys out to war. All of the Blue Angels volunteered to serve in Korea. In 1949, the team had flown 51 shows. The Korean War cut this schedule down to only 22. The last airshows flown before deploying for Korean War duties were July 9 at NAS Glenview, July 20 at NAS Pensacola, and two airshows at Dallas on July 29 and 30. The team left Dallas, heading for San Diego on July 31. The following day, the

Blue Angels delivered their aircraft and reported in at NAS Moffett Field.

Upon arrival, the Blues formed the nucleus of VF-191 as the squadron transferred over to jets. VF-191 had recently returned from a cruise on the USS *Boxer* (CVA-21), flying F8F Bearcats. The air group was based at NAS Alameda, and VF-191 was based at Moffett, which until the arrival of VF-191, had been a transport and night-fighter base. VF-191 was the first squadron of jet-powered fighter aircraft to be based at Moffett. The squadron transitioned into the jets and deployed aboard the USS *Princeton* (CV-37) in only two months. Robcke recalled the work-up:

We carrier qualified on the *Princeton* on October 16–20, 1950. On November 7, we flew our birds to Alameda, and they were loaded on board the *Princeton*. We arrived NAS Barbers Point, Hawaii, on November 15. On November 22, the squadron flew out to the ship and headed for the waters off Korea.

Korea, for the first cruise, was not all that exciting. It was exciting from the fact that we were getting shot at fairly frequently. Jets were new to carriers in those days. We had an excellent ship, the *Princeton*, although they were a little afraid of the airplanes. Any time we had jets in the air, one of the senior squadron officers had to be in primary flight control up on the island. If we did not have enough wind, they would cancel the jets. They did not know what to do with us really. We flew a lot of CAP [Combat Air Patrol] and frankly did not do much flying at all.

During the month of December, I only flew 17 hours flying off the ship; January, only 7.1; February, a mere 3.5; 12.5 in March; 12 in April; and 13 in May. We flew photo escorts, attacked tanks, armed reconnaissance. We flew a lot of reconnaissance—looking for the bad guys.

## The Blues Lose a Leader

Robcke's log-book entry for March 8, 1951, reads:

"Skipper crashed off Korean east coast near Tanchon. Aircraft burning from AA hit during strafing run." LCdr. Johnny Magda was the first Blue Angels leader to die in combat.

His wingman got some fantastic gun camera pictures. He saw that the airplane was on fire, and he was yelling at Magda to get out. He eventually got behind him, and using his gun camera he got some pictures. You can see that the whole bottom of the aircraft was on fire. I think he did get out right at the last minute.

But Magda did not make it.

VF-191 returned stateside to Moffett Field in June 1951.

## Second Korean Tour

When deploying for the first cruise, the Blue Angels turned in their aircraft for overhaul because they were not fleet-configured. After the cruise, the squadron returned to Moffett Field and reformed. When they went out on the second cruise, two or three of the original airshow airplanes went with them.

By March 1952, VF-191 was back aboard USS *Princeton*. Robcke described the action:

By this time they were used to the jets, and they were using us a lot more. Near the end of this cruise, we started escorting the prop strike groups. They would launch the props [Skyraiders] for the beach about an hour before the jets. We would catch them just as they got to the beach. (By then they started hanging stuff on our airplanes. We had four 20mm cannons in the nose, and they would put one proximity-fused fragmentation bomb and four rockets under each wing.) We would go in first and strafe from real high up in a steep dive, then pick up the lead for the rockets and fire a pair of those, and then pickle a bomb off just before we pulled out. We would then zoom up and catch the last prop entering its dive. To the best of my knowledge, no prop was ever hit [by anti-aircraft fire] when we provided flack suppression.

VF-191 returned from Korea on October 17, 1952.

One of the first photos taken of the team flying the F9F-5.
The -5 suffered from fuel-control problems that delayed the
start of the 1952 season until June. Once the problem was solved,
the -5 proved to be an excellent airshow mount.
*Grumman History Center*

# Chapter Three

# Restarting the Team After Korea

Butch Voris was in Washington at the time, in the Bureau of Aeronautics. He headed up the Pratt & Whitney engine development desk, and on November 1, 1950, he received a phone call from a friend. He told Voris that the Secretary of the Navy wanted to get the Blue Angels reformed immediately. Voris was asked to spend the weekend writing up the requirements to restart the team—aircraft, manpower, support, and so on.

"They had asked me to recommend pilots who had been on the team before; who would return to the team," Voris said. "I didn't recommend a leader because I felt it was not in my position to recommend someone." Soon after submitting his report, Voris got a call commending him for his work, but that he had failed to name a leader. The Navy wanted Voris to lead the team again. He was married now and knew he had to ask his wife, Thea, before he accepted the position. Not knowing how his wife would react, they set up a cocktail party to break the decision to Mrs. Voris. Voris described the setup:

> There were several admirals there, and one of them in particular, who had a responsiblity for this whole thing, was Adm. Bringle. We were out on this screen porch sipping martinis. It was a setup. Thea's out there, and we're all in a circle, and Adm. Bringle says "Butch, we'd like to have you come back and start the team again." I said, "Like I told you, I've been there once; it's someone else's turn." Thea looked at me and said, "What's the matter? Are you afraid?" That's all it took. I told her afterwards that we had pulled a setup on her, but within 10 days we were in Corpus Christi. We had to move.

Lt. Pat Murphy and LCdr. Ray Hawkins were the two veteran Blue Angel pilots who returned to form the nucleus of the new team. The team was reunited with the Panther, although this time with F9F-5s powered by J-48-P-6 engines. The Bearcat also returned to the team, but only briefly. The advance-man/narrator flew the plane, but it was incompatible with the jets, and parts were hard to obtain. "We had to get the advance-man something compatible to fly," said Voris, "so we requested the Lockheed TO-2. He gave press rides and would go out a couple of days in advance of the team to make sure that everything was set up—hotels, all the things we would need from the airshow authority. So the TO-2 worked out well. It had a long range with the two tip tanks, and the back seat for rides."

Cdr. R. M. "Butch" Voris was selected to reform the team after the break-up for Korea. Voris is standing in a new Grumman F9F-5 Panther. *Voris collection*

## The F7U-1 Cutlass and F9F-5 Teething Problems

LCdr. E. L. "Whitey" Feightner was a test pilot at NAS Patuxent River. He was a combat veteran and had an excellent reputation as an engineering test pilot. Feightner was given the nickname "Whitey" by Cdr. E. H. "Butch" O'Hare. "I was in Butch's squadron [VF-3] right after he became a big ace in World War II," said Feightner. "He was a great spear fisherman. He used to take the whole squadron out to go spear fishing. Everybody in the squadron got tan, except for me. Everybody thought it was because of my hair, but it really wasn't. It was just the fact that I didn't tan. So they nicknamed me 'Whitey.'"

At Patuxent River, Feightner was evaluating the pre-production Vought F7U-1 Cutlass. This radical aircraft design was a high-speed, tail-less jet, powered by two afterburning J-34 engines capable of 4,250 pounds thrust each. (Later production models would be powered by the 4,600-pound-thrust Westinghouse J-46-WE-8). The plane had an extended nose gear placing the cockpit 12 feet above the ground. The F7U had another peculiar feature—a two-position landing gear. The main gear had one position for landing and another for takeoff. For takeoff, the pilot had to shift it forward about 18 inches to give enough airflow over the elevators to lift the nose wheel off. On landing, the gear automatically returned back 18 inches. Once the nose wheel touched, the pilot would not have enough speed to get it off again until well over 150 knots.

The Blue Angels could not fly the F7U in formation because it was the first operational airplane the Navy flew that had a hydraulic control system. The hydraulic system was backed up by a mechanical one, but it was not all that foolproof. Feightner said of the system:

We used to lose it a lot. It would fail an awful lot of times. When it did, it took 11 seconds before the mechanical control system took over and you could control the airplane. That's three life times! Believe me.

I have made the claim, and I think it is probably still good today, that I have the most passenger time in single-place airplanes of any guy living. I've spent a lot of time waiting for that 11 seconds to expire. This thing was a spectacular airshow airplane—as long as you could fly it singly.

We got two F7U-1s ready in January 1952 and went down to Corpus Christi to be part of the team. I got orders to the team, and I went with them. These were new airplanes right out of the plant. We configured them especially for the Blue Angels. We left out anything they did not need, such as guns, ammo cans, anything that was excess weight.

Now, the Blue Angels had two new radical jet fighters, but only one pilot. Feightner had known Lt. "Mac" MacKnight, a Blue Angel from the 1948–49 team. MacKnight was in the training command and was not happy about it. Feightner approached MacKnight on rejoining the team and learning to fly the Cutlass. MacKnight quickly agreed. Soon after, Feightner put on a memorable one-man airshow in the F7U:

We got the airplanes down to Corpus Christi, and I started to get MacKnight checked out in them. Then the F9F-5s got grounded, and we did not have any airplanes. We put the team in TV-2s, Lockheed Shooting Stars. I flew in the

F7U in the first few shows. MacKnight did not have enough time to fly in the shows.

The team flew people around in the TV-2s, and one of the biggest demonstrations we had was at Pensacola. That was a Secretary of the Navy cruise where he had all of the top industrial people, company presidents, and others down there for a cruise out on the carrier. I gave them an airshow while we were there. The team flew those that wanted to fly; they put them in the back seat of the TVs and took them up for a flight around the Pensacola area. I put on the show at Sofley Field. That turned out to be a spectacular event. I made a takeoff and hit the afterburners. The airplane was going straight up,

and just about the time I passed 200 feet, I lost the control system.

The airplane went ballistic and arced up. At about 1,200 to 1,500 feet, it ran out of speed, the nose dropped through, and I'm still unconnected, still riding at this point. I never got high enough to eject, because you did not dare eject anywhere below 1,000 feet because you would not make it. So I was just sitting there watching the ground come up at me. Finally, everything connected up; the airplane did about a square turn—and there's a little debate about whether the wheels touched the ground or not. By this time, I was so low that I could not get over the trees at the end of the field, so I carved a hole through them. When I did that,

The new team was formed with (left to right) Tom Jones, Voris as leader, Pat Murphy, Ray Hawkins (who flew with the team prior to Korea), and Buddy Rich. Hawkins would relieve Voris as team leader in January 1953. *Voris collection*

Navy and aircraft contractor politics forced a pair of pre-production F7U-1 Cutlasses on the team. The unusual, tail-less design featured afterburners and one of the fastest roll rates of a Naval fighter up to that time. The planes were a maintenance nightmare and were flown only during the 1952 season. *John M. Campbell collection*

it tore off the port slat. That went down the port intake, and I lost the port engine. This was a really gusty day. I got the engine shut down OK. The engine fire warning light went out, and I came around and declared an emergency.

The minute you put the landing gear down with a single engine on this bird, it was landed. It would not stay airborne. I got around; they cleared the field for me, and I dropped the landing gear. It was a little hairy, but I got it on the ground alright. I rolled up to the crowd standing there, and everybody was very quiet. They were waiting to see how I was going to get out of the airplane. There was no ladder and I was sitting 12 feet off the ground. They watched me climb out of the airplane, jump down, and a big cheer went up.

About that time Adm. Price, who was head of the Training Command, came over and congratulated me. Then he said, "I really feel terrible about this, but will the other airplane fly?" So I immediately got in the other airplane and finished putting on an airshow for them.

The F9F-5s arrived from Grumman in late January or early February but were not ungrounded until June. The planes were having fuel-control problems. They used to give fire warning lights all the time. Voris would be leading the team, just get inverted, and someone's fire warning light would come on. The team finally decided to disconnect the fire warning lights. They figured there were enough people watching them that if they did catch fire, they would soon hear about it.

While the team was grounded, Feightner and MacKnight showed the Blue Angels' colors, accompanied by Lt. Buddy Rich in an F9F-5. "We did that between March and June when the F9F-5s got ungrounded," Feightner said. "The team got enough F9F-5s ungrounded that they could practice, but they could not put on a show.

Meanwhile, Feightner continued testing the F7U's limits:

[The F7U had] the fastest rate of roll of any airplane the Navy's ever had, before or since. I was doing some of the tests in the F7U, and I have an instrumented roll in which I did an average, over the five turns, of 576 degrees per second. I've never seen a guy who could throw the stick over in that airplane and stop it upright. I used to use that feature in the airshows. It also had the best set of speed brakes on it ever invented. Absolutely no trim change when you threw them out. They stopped you like you had just caught the arresting gear.

After I got MacKnight trained in the F7U, we used to come at each other doing about 450 from opposite sides of the runway, each one of us on the right side of the runway centerline, and just as we passed each other, we would throw out the speed brakes and hit the afterburner. We would never cross the far end of the field. We would just do square turns and fly down past each other going in the opposite direction. There just is not an airplane like it anywhere.

One of the things that stopped the F7U as an airshow act was an incident during an airshow for the South Western Conference of High Schools. It was one of those Blue Northern days down in Texas. The ceiling was 800 feet or so, absolutely clear underneath, but the clouds were really low. Feightner went up to put on a flat show doing turns and rolls and, once again, barely survived an airshow in the Cutlass:

I had a maneuver that I had worked out where I would do full aileron rolls to the left, and because of the high rate of roll, the horizon would play tricks in my mind. At that high rate of speed, if you roll the airplane more than a couple of turns, the horizon is flipping back and forth about 40 degrees. You don't know where the horizon is. I had found out that if I did about three turns to the left and reversed it a full throw going the other direction three turns, it would counteract it and the horizon would be still for me.

I went into my three turns to the left. I was in the middle of the maneuver, when a little light plane popped out of the overcast. I was right in front of the grandstand at this point. I shoved forward on the stick, flew straight up into the overcast and missed the guy somehow. They tell me my wake turned that guy over completely when I went by. The negative-g pull-up overstressed the airplane so much that it tore off the landing gear doors. Big pieces of the doors went all through the crowd because I was rolling at the time. Fortunately, nobody got hurt. They picked up pieces about the size of your fist that had come off the airplane. It also tore off one of the slats and, again, I lost one of the engines. That's the sort of thing we kept running into.

The plane was a maintenance nightmare. Lt. Bob Belt, the maintenance officer, used to tear his hair out over this airplane and its hydraulic system. In the middle of getting ready for the season, the Navy decided to change from red hydraulic fluid to Hytrol, which was a non-flammable type of fluid. "The only thing was," Feightner recalled, "they forgot to stress how much the system had to be flushed. The little bit of hydraulic fluid that was left mixed with the new Hytrol, and it just made a kind of gunk. So we had to completely strip the hydraulic system from the airplane and reinstall it. We had Vought representatives that did all of the work, but it did cause a lot of consternation."

Those who flew the F7U all agreed that it was a "pretty hairy airplane." The final straw that ended the F7U-1's tenure with the team came on a trip to the opening of the new Pittsburgh Airport. Feightner and MacKnight left Corpus Christi and headed for St. Louis for fuel. Like all of the early jets, the F7U was short-legged. After departing St. Louis, MacKnight had a hydraulic problem, and was forced to land at Columbus, Ohio. Feightner continued on to Pittsburgh. MacKnight arrived

the next day. The pair flew one fly-over, and then the aircraft were on static display for the airport's open house. They had a small problem and had to have a new engine flown in. After the engine change, the pair got ready to depart for a show at NAS Glenview. Feightner recalled the trip:

It was raining the morning we took off. I lost an engine shortly after takeoff when we were climbing up. With a single engine, I wasn't about to go back and make an instrument approach. So we headed on for Glenview. I got over Glenview and declared a deferred emergency, but instructed them that once I put the landing gear down I had to land. I couldn't go around any more. I circled a minute while they got the crash crews out there. MacKnight and I came across the airport at about 1,500 feet doing about 300 knots, headed for the lake. Directly over the center of the field, MacKnight said he had a fire warning light on the right engine. Then he called back, "Whoops, there goes the left one." I turned around to see what had happened and I said, "The minute we're over the water, you eject." About that time I saw MacKnight inverted, flaming like mad, and headed down. He actually split-S'd that airplane from 1,500 feet. There is no other jet in the world you could split-S from 1,500—that I know of. He got away with it.

I caught up with him just as he was going over the fence onto the airport and had him blow the gear down. He was really flaming. At that point, just as the main gear touched down, I saw the nose gear come out and lock. The minute the nose gear hit the runway, MacKnight went over the side—parachute and all. He went over the left side from 12 feet in the air doing about 80 knots. He rolled off that wing and across the tarmac and the airplane went out and did about a half ground loop and stopped. The crash crew came over and put out the fire.

After that, we had to take a good look at the airplane. The mechanics from Corpus Christi came up there. I took the R5C and went down and picked up a bunch of the Vought crew and four new engines for the airplanes. We headed back for Glenview, but not without a little bit of a mishap. I was climbing out of Dallas after one of these Blue Northerns had gone through. The wind was blowing about 40 knots, and the day was absolutely

Vought F7U-1 BuNo. 124426, Blue Angel No. 7, on display at NAS Glenview. Both of the Cutlasses declared emergencies on final to Glenview prior to the show. *Clay Jansson via Larkins*

clear. At 9,000 feet, both engines on that R5C quit. I had a chief in there with me, so I had everybody get into their parachute harnesses. We could not get any fuel pressure, absolutely zero. So we turned around and were headed back towards Dallas when we decided we would get out at 5,000 feet. About that point the chief was flying while I was getting into my harness. He said, "Commander, I can see the field from here. We can make it." I looked and sure enough, that wind had really blown us back toward the airport. I made the decision and instructed the chief to tell the guys that anybody who wanted to jump could, but I was going to take the airplane in and try to land it. I gave the chief the same option. He went back and talked to the passengers. He returned and said everybody was going to stick with it. We dead-sticked it into Dallas.

It took them 10 minutes to find out that somebody had not tightened the clamp on the main fuel line, a big 3.5-inch line, and it had just fallen off. They fixed it and we were ready to go. I went in to file the flight plan and told the chief to get the crew loaded; we would be going in a little bit. He returned and said, "Those guys are at Love Field. They are going to take an airliner to Chicago."

Once back at Glenview, we found out that we could fix both of the airplanes. The fire had not done that much damage to MacKnight's airplane—it was primarily fuel and hydraulic fuel burning. There was just a little sheet-metal work

that had to be done. The planes were fixed, and we were ready to go. I decided to take the repaired airplane and put Mac in the airplane I'd been flying—it only had one new engine in it. Mac took it up to break in the new engine on a test flight. He put the gear handle down and the landing gear lowered—one in the landing position and one in the forward position.

When they got ahold of me and told me of his problem, I ran out on the field. There was a Marine taxiing by in an F8F. I jumped on the wing and convinced him to get out and give me his airplane—which he did. (I never found the guy to thank him.) He got out of the airplane, and I climbed in and went up to look at Mac's predicament. By flying underneath, I could see that both gear were locked, so I gave MacKnight the option, he could either try to land it that way or bail out. Nobody had ever landed one like that before, but he opted to land it. It worked like a charm. We checked it, and I test-hopped it. The gear turned out to be alright, and we headed for Memphis.

We were going to meet the team there for their first show. The F9F-5s were ready to go. We flew on down and near Memphis; MacKnight started to lose hydraulic fluid. I could finally see it pouring out of his airplane. By this time he was on the mechanical system, and we declared an emergency. He landed on the runway, and it was just one big sheet of hydraulic fluid behind him. I landed shortly thereafter, and we had a conference with Bob Belt. He just gave up on the airplane. He could not maintain them any more. We gave them up to the training center at Memphis, and they used them as test beds for their mechanics. They never left there.

By that time, Patuxent River wanted me back to fly the F7U-3. Since I was the only one to ever fly an F7U-1 aboard ship, they wanted me back to take the F7U-3 aboard.

## Tragedy Strikes Again

Now that the Cutlasses had been deleted from the Blue Angels routine, and the F9F-5s were ungrounded, it was time to get on with the season.

Each year, the midshipmen from Annapolis go on a summer cruise. In 1952, some of them came to Corpus Christi for their aviation-indoctrination summer cruise. They arrived on board the USS *Constitution*. For two weeks, they went around to the various hangars, listened to lectures, and talked with the pilots. The Blue Angels were slated to perform for them. Bleachers were set up on the concrete seaplane ramp, but the show was delayed for a day because a Blue Northern came through—turbulence, thunderstorms, no possibility of flying the show. The midshipmen were given rides on the ground. Pilots would stand on the side of the airplane and let

the midshipmen start up the jets and taxi on the seaplane ramp.

The next day broke gusty, but clear. Voris advised the team to watch their step during the airshow. The team was going to perform along the mile-long seaplane ramp. Whitey Feightner was manning the ground-control radio. It was his last day as a Blue Angel. He was detaching from the team after the show. Feightner's duties were to maintain contact with the formation over the team frequency. He would feed the announcer the team's next maneuver.

Voris led the Diamond formation, Ray Hawkins on the left wing, Pat Murphy on the right, and Lt. Bud Wood flying slot. The team took off and lined up for their entry on the show site. The four Panther jets dove down, picking up speed for their opening pass. The team rolled left, presenting the underside of the aircraft to the midshipmen, showing the US Navy lettering on the jet's wings. Hawkins was probably no more than 100 feet off the deck. The formation then pulled up into a chandelle turn and reversed back in for a series of vertical maneuvers. Voris described that day:

It kept getting a little bumpier and I kept saying, "Ease it out; ease it out."

Now, when we could and the weather per-

Lt. Roland P. "Auz" Asland's F9F-5, BuNo. 125305, at Oakland February 15, 1953. *William T. Larkins*

mitted, the wing of the wingman would ride behind the leader's wing, but ahead of his stabilizer. It would actually work in that pocket. It was tight, very tight. The No. 4 man flew directly underneath, looking up at the tail skag of the leader. The reason for this was to get up ahead of the wash coming off the leader so it would not interfere with them aerodynamically. So, here we are, almost a vertical turn, flying over 400 knots, pulling no more than 2 g's, when I got a pretty good jolt. I said, "Lets move it out, move it out." I caught a flash of Hawkins' wing coming up right in that little pocket. If he slides aft, there goes my tail, if he goes forward there goes my wing. We had to separate, move it out.

The next thing that I knew was this horrendous crash. Hawkins' wing came up and took off my port side horizontal stabilizer and elevator, everything went. This kicked me over and I came down on top of Bud Wood and took off his nose. His CG [center of gravity] rolled aft and he pulled up and ejected right in front of the crowd. A crowd of midshipmen we were going to convince that aviation was the way to go. Wood was not high enough to get out of his seat, so he was still strapped in when he hit the water. It was a bad day. This was a pretty low spot.

I red out. Absolutely the prettiest shade of Chinese red you ever saw. You're not unconscious, but you can't see. I figured I'd had a catastrophic engine failure, that's what first crossed my mind. Then I realized that wasn't it. I had over-temp lights on, I pulled to idle automatically.

When I could see again, I remember that I was level with palm trees. On my left side was Gold Coast Row, where all the admirals lived. On the radio I'm hearing Whitey Feightner saying, "Butch, get out, get out." In that day the seats were gunpowder charged and you had to be at at least 2,000 feet before you had enough altitude to get out, get out of your seat, get the parachute to open, and land. I couldn't get out.

I remember crossing the O-Club swimming pool. The things you remember. I can remember who was parked there.

I get the nose to start up through residual speed. It's vibrating like hell. Over-temp lights are on. The tail-pipe out gauge is right up against the blocks of temperature limitations. I know I'm having to hold right stick all the way over, but the rudder is jammed. When I got Bud Wood's nose, his nose came up and carried into my rudder and jammed it full right. All this time I am gaining altitude. I have started putting the power on. I am at the maximum limitation according to my tail-pipe out gauge, but I had no alternative. If it's going to blow up, it's going to blow up.

I got through 2,000 feet and figured if I had to, I could get out now. The seats were not as dependable in those years. Meanwhile, Whitey is still saying, "Get out Butch; you're going to get a reversal on your controls; get out over the water." I figured that I could slow down to about 200 knots, and I remember going just under 220 and starting to lose control. So back up to 230 I went.

## Feightner recalled his view from the ground:

The bottom of the pass was at 1,500 feet or so. Just as they started pulling out, pieces started flying, and all four airplanes came together. Butch was in real trouble. He had no down elevator. He was unable to get the canopy open—in those days you could not eject through the canopy, so he was sort of stuck. He had to set the airplane down some place, and I got on the horn with the tower and decided to send him over to NAS Kingsville because they have a nice, long runway where he could land. In the meantime, I had talked to Butch enough to find out that he could slow it enough to put it on the runway with power. Since he could not get out, he had no other choice. He had to do it.

## Back to Voris in the cockpit:

I was going to try for Kingsville's 10,000-foot runway, straight in. I've got the rest of my team around me. Hawkins has three feet of his wing missing and Murphy's lost his tip tank. I just headed straight in, no flaps, of course. They told me, Hawkins and Murphy, "Your fuselage is split; we can see right through it." I don't know what held the two halves together. It just beats me. I just kept going straight and could see this concrete runway out ahead of me. I went through 2,000 feet and thought, *This is it; you've got to go ahead or you're dead.* I

The team's public information officer, LCdr. Frank Graham, flew TV-2 BuNo. 128676, Blue Angel No. "0". By late 1953, the plane's scheme included checkered nose and wing tips.  Photo shot at NRAB Oakland, California.
*William T. Larkins*

went in and landed, and I got it stopped within 10,000 feet. I did not shut off the engine because I think shock set in. In the air you are busy working, but on the ground I was down. I actually taxied up to the flight line. The crash trucks and ambulance were there. I got out of the airplane and was definitely in a state of shock by that time.

In the meantime, they had sent the admiral's R4D out to get us and take us back to Adm. Morehouse. We got the other two planes down, and then had to get to the wives. My wife was in California at that time. The police had already found her downtown and informed her there was a crash of the Blue Angels. We got to all of the wives to let them know we lost Bud Wood. His wife was there. We tried to console her.

We had to rebuild just as quickly as we could. We got three new airplanes, got them repainted, and we were back in the air in less than two weeks. Bud Rich came up to take Wood's place. We went on from there. You have got to get back on the horse. You have a little hollow in the pit of your stomach when you take the team out again, but I started them off at a couple thousand feet, a couple of rolls, and then we went right back at it.

On September 17, 1952, the team performed at the dedication of Whiting Field's Magda Village, a base housing unit named in honor of team leader Johnny Magda. The last show of the season was flown at Barin Field, Florida.

Ray Hawkins took over the team in January 1953. Hawkins' team consisted of Lieutenants Pat Murphy, Dayl Crow, Auz Ausland, Bud Rich, and Frank Jones. They introduced the Left Echelon Roll during the show at New Orleans in late January. Also, the R4D support plane was replaced by a Curtiss R5C-1 from the pool at NAS Corpus Christi.

## Blue Angels Consider Moving Up to a Swept-Wing Cat

The successful Panther design had been given swept wings and other modifications by Grumman and was renamed the Cougar. In the effort to fly the Navy's latest, the team planned to transition to the new, swept-wing F9F-6 Cougar. The team picked up six new F9F-6 Cougars from the Grumman plant at Bethpage in August 1953. This model was the first aircraft in the Navy's inventory to have a flying tail—where the stabilizer and elevator are one unit and move as such.

During the flight from Bethpage to Corpus Christi, on August 4, team leader Hawkins' flying tail began to leak hydraulic pressure from the underside of a cylinder. The cylinder's push rod locked, sending the Cougar into a nose dive. Hawkins recalled the ride:

When I reached over to cut the flying tail, it did a complete outside loop, it went all the way under. I was redding out, blood rushing to my head. I had to bail out through the canopy because I was so squished up under the negative g's that I could not get the center of the handle all the way down to blow the canopy off.

We had a new way, in this particular airplane, to arm the seat. I just armed it and blew myself through the plexiglass canopy. My plane was traveling above the speed of sound when I went out. The problem started at about 42,000, and it was 32,000 feet when I got out. When I hit the slipstream and it blew everything off—oxygen mask, helmet, goggles. I was hanging there with no oxygen. I grunt breathed, which is something the Navy teaches you in training. Whereas the oxygen is up there, the pressure is not there to force it into your lungs. I would take a deep breath and grunt, trying to force pressure into my lungs as best I could. That forces a little oxygen into your blood—enough to keep you alive. When I got down to 15,000 feet, I was OK then. I landed near Pickins, Mississippi.

The F9F-6s were never flown in an airshow by the Blue Angels. After Hawkins' accident, the aircraft were returned to the factory to have a manual override built into the flying-tail system. They were then dispersed to the fleet. The Blues kept flying the Panther until the end of the 1954 season.

In September 1953, the R5C-1 was replaced with a Douglas R4D-8 Super Skytrain. This aircraft would serve until the end of 1955. At the end of the year and into January 1954, the team went to Jacksonville to participate in the filming of *Cinerama*. Hawkins said the team flew a couple of Diamond Rolls, but mainly the film-makers were looking for one shot. The producers set the camera up in the middle of the runway, and "we flew right at the camera at about 150 feet or so, as low as you could. They filmed us coming at them and then had us come back the other way for the away shot. The end result, if you were sitting in the movie theater, was that the four airplanes came right at you and if you ducked, when you looked back at the screen, you saw them flying away. There were only about two maneuvers used in the movie plus the fly-by scene right over the camera."

Cdr. R. L. "Zeke" Cormier took over as team leader on February 21, 1954, at NAS New Orleans, when he relieved Ray Hawkins. Here Cormier leads the team over El Centro, California. *Zeke Cormier*

## The Aerial Change of Command Ceremony

Ray Hawkins had put the Fleur de Lis into the routine. When looking at the flower, the petals split off to the left and to the right, with one up straight ahead. Hawkins described the maneuver:

From the Diamond formation, we would pull up as if we were going into a loop. Just as the formation is at about vertical, everybody splits and does a roll. Right wingman half rolls and splits off to the right, left wingman half rolls to the left and splits off, while the slot man rolls in position. The leader continues in his loop, and everybody else continues in their loops. They join in the Diamond at the bottom.

Cmdr. R. L. "Zeke" Cormier was slated to relieve Hawkins as the officer in charge of the Blue Angels. The aerial change-of-command ceremony took place on February 21, 1954, during the show at NAS New Orleans. Hawkins had modified the Fleur de Lis for a dynamic change-of-command ceremony. He described the maneuver:

All we did was tuck the new leader, Zeke Cormier, in behind the slot man thus forming an arrow. When we started to pull up, Cormier pulled up first from his trail position. He then headed up into the loop, and as we reached the point of break, Cormier was just about to start down from his loop. My three wingmen had broken from me, I went on up, over the loop and rolled out, as if in a Cuban Eight, but I rolled out on top. The three wingmen went on around and joined Cormier on the bottom.

## Zeke Cormier Finishes Out the Panther Years

Zeke Cormier described how the Blue Angels were selected at the time he came on board:

A friend of mine was on the staff, and we had flown together during World War II. I wanted to go to the team when they first put it together in Jacksonville, so I applied. I was on the West Coast and Jacksonville is on the East Coast, and in those days Atlantic [fleet] guys did not talk to Pacific [fleet] guys. So I could not get orders to go to Jacksonville. As it turned out, I went back in the squadron I flew in the war with, and went back out on a WestPac [Western Pacific cruise]. So I missed that opportunity.

The selection process was more informal in those days. The guy who is leading the team could say, "Here is some guy I think you should consider and his availability, and this is my recommendation." And the chief of Naval Air Training, through his chief of staff, would talk to the Blues' skipper, and then they would pick him.

When Cormier became skipper of the Blues, he selected Lt. Ed McKellar and later Lt. Nello Pierozzi to join the team. When Cormier came on there were five pilots, four in the formation and one solo. The solo would make passes while the formation regrouped for the next maneuver. He described his changes to the routines:

I wanted to make it symmetrical. One solo from each direction. So we added the sixth airplane. [McKellar was added as the opposing solo.]

We made several changes to the show starting in 1954. First of all, I thought it was too long. I'd rather do it quick, fast-paced, and get the audience asking for more. So we cut it down to 17 minutes. It finally grew back to 20 minutes, but that was as much time as we put into it. We changed the opening, a couple vertical maneuvers, and added the Tuck Under Break. We left in the tried and true maneuvers like the Diamond Roll, the Echelon Roll, and the tight breaks close in. We started landing in formation, which was new. It was dangerous as hell, and I don't know how we got away with it all those years. The Navy asked if we could do it. We said we could, and that was the end of it. It was pretty hair-raising. You always run the risk of somebody blowing a tire and then being unable to control the airplane on the ground.

We were the first team to go to El Centro to train during the winter season. When I took over the team at Corpus Christi, Texas, the weather was absolutely miserable. We fiddled around there trying to get some flights in. I went to my boss, Adm. Glover, and asked what he thought about taking the team and going to El Centro. The weather's great, there is nobody there; essentially, in those days, it had been abandoned and was in a caretaker status. We would have the whole place to ourselves, and we could practice right over the field. He thought it was a great idea. So we packed up everything and moved to El Centro. We could fly two or three hops a day and do it six days a week. The best part was that my family was out on the West Coast.

We spent a month at El Centro. Our first show was at El Centro; our next one was at NARB New Orleans. My ultimate boss, Adm. John Dell Price, came over to see the show. He thought it was great. He liked the change of some of the new maneuvers and thought the Fleur de Lis was great.

Blue Angel No. 5 at NRAB Oakland, California, September 25, 1954. Note the Grumman AF-2S Guardian behind F9F-5's nose. *Harrison W. Rued*

The second TV-2 to join the Blue Angels was BuNo. 128662, seen here at the San Francisco International Airport Airshow on August 28, 1954. *William T. Larkins*

Cormier's team flew the Panthers as they were, but later on had to make some changes, as he recalled:

> We were flying with 150-gallon tip tanks, and what we did, before we got into airshow smoke, was to add fuel die, blue in one side and red in the other. When we would do the maneuvers, we would just dump the fuel. It got all over the cars and the crowd. So we had to stop that.
>
> Then we got into the smoke generator [first year, 1955]. All we did was put a tank of automobile motor oil inside the airplane and ran a tube back and stuck it in the tail pipe. When we would go with the smoke, we would just turn on the switch and the oil would flow back into the tail pipe and would vaporize it. That gave us a really white billowing smoke.

Cormier's 1954 team was the first to open a position to a US Marine Corps flying officer. At least one position has been reserved for a Marine ever since.

One of the most important members of the team is the public affairs officer. Cormier's man,

During the 1954 season the team was supported by this R4D-8 Super Skytrain, BuNo. 12437, photographed at Oakland, October 1954. Note the team's F9F-5s under the wing and propeller of the R4D-8. *William T. Larkins*

LCdr. Dick Newhafer had a real flair for public affairs. Said Cormier:

> Media rides were something we wanted to do. Each place we stopped, they picked an aviation writer or some guy who was doing a PR piece on the local airshow. Newhafer would fly them in the TV-1. He would fly them locally, kind of a gentle

# Ode To The Blues

**This tribute to the Blue Angels was written by LCdr. Dick Newhafer, narrator for Cdr. Zeke Cormier's 1954–55 team.**

The crowd stood dazed in the morning air,
In an icy death grip held;
And from the bowels of the milling throng,
An awesome murmur swelled.
It rose and strained in the blowing wind,
And hammered against the sky;
And shouted its word to the firmament,
The BLUES were going to fly. . .

And who were these sky-born eagles then,
Who fancied that man-made wings,
Could lift them in loops and Cuban Eights,
And changeover rolls and things?
Could hold those thousands spellbound there,
Dead still in the morning sun;
As the Arch Fear wondered himself at length,
At the things that were being done . . .

Well, the man in front flying number one,
Was a fearsome thing at best;
With a face as black as the bowels of hell,
And a head like a hornet's nest;
A mouth all teeth in that awesome face,
A forehead an ape would spurn;
A matted chest like an afghan rug,
And a nose like a mangled "gern". . .

As they came to the crowd from the rising sun,
Like an eagle swarm from the east;
The kid that was flying the number two,
Had a head like a polish priest;
Some seventy pounds that big head weighed,
And shaped in a perfect cube;
This throwback to Neolithic man,
Was known as "The Iron Tale"...

And floundering under the port-side wing,
Like a kangaroo in heat;
Jerking the throttle, fighting the stick,
Bounding within his seat,
Sat Denmark's gift to the Angels Blue,
Whose beauty will long be sung;
'Twas Golden Boy with his flaxen hair,
And eyes that were filled with Wung . . .

While wallowing under the Black Thing's tail,
With a ferret face of a rat;
A bottle of vodka on his lap,
The Tennessee Colonel sat;
Flying the difficult number four,
Position that's known as the slot,
The Colonel certainly made it so,
Whether it was or not . . .

And so they came to the waiting throng,
Who stood like a breathless sea;
And burst like a petal in perfect grace,
In the fabulous Fleur de Lis;
The crowd stood fixed in a breathless stare,
And watched in frozen awe;
What happened then was the goddamnedest thing,
That anyone ever saw . . .

For someone goofed at the top of the loop,
And headings became divergent;
And Cormier crashed in a sheet of flame,
Like a volatile detergent;
The Golden Boy flew out the West,
The last time he was seen;
While the Tube and Colonel side by side,
Finally landed in Moline . . .

So the Blues go blun and the work was done,
And buddy . . . if you'd ask me,
The thing that finally busted their ass
Was that goddamn Fleur de Lis . . .

ride. He would give them some general information about the team, and it would appear in the newspaper. That's how we got our PR. Normally Newhafer would show up one day in advance and leave one day afterward so he could bring all of the news clips. We kept a log of all of our media coverage. We were really getting into the PR aspect of the Blues about that time. Newhafer

was replaced by Lt. Bruce Bagwell. Bagwell was a first class PR guy. He knew how to speak to the media and select the guys to ride in the airplane; he just was outstanding.

During this time period, Grumman had been working to steadily improve the Cougar. The F9F-6 gave way to the vastly improved F9F-8.

The 1956 season was the last for the TV-2.
Here the public information officer's TV-2 No. 0
wears the Naval Air Training Command banner on its tip tanks.
The plane is seen at Oakland, August 1956.
*Harrison W. Rued*

# Chapter Four

# Enter the Cougar

In December, after the end of the 1954 season, the Blue Angels began transition training in the F9F-8 Cougar. The team transitioned into the Cougar with ease. They had a small accident in late 1954, when two F9F-5s bumped, knocking off both wing tip tanks. The F9F-8s were clean-winged, and the absence of tip tanks made things a little easier.

Team leader Cormier remembered:

The 8 had a great deal more power than the -5. It was an easier airplane to fly. We did not get as much proximity effect. The air flowing over the surfaces of the aircraft create a barrier, if you will. In the -5s, the wingmen would form up and they would have to put their wing in between my wing, the tail, and the fuselage. The tip tank brought the planes closer together by several inches. As the leader, I would look out the side and see that tip tank sitting in my hip pocket.

The proximity effect gave the wingmen the feeling that they were creeping into the formation. They would have to hold outboard stick to keep the wing from edging closer and closer to the flight leader. The slot man would slip up underneath everybody, and you would get this feeling that your nose was coming up—and it was. The leader had to keep the nose down to stay straight. If we wanted to do a vertical maneuver, like going into a loop, the lead pilot would just relax the stick pressure, and the flight would start to nose up. You could almost fly it hands off in the -5. We had the same effect in the -8, but not to the extent we did in the -5. You still got the proximity effect of the slot pilot slipping up under the lead. You wanted him to be there on all the vertical maneuvers because if he got behind the curve, he got left, and he did not have enough power on the plane to catch up. If he got behind in a vertical maneuver you really got in trouble. Before we would start the maneuver, he would close up so we could get a run at it. Those little tricks you learn as you go through the training cycle are important. When you are flying three hops a day, six days a week, you get to know the airplane pretty well and what you can do and what you can't.

Lieutenant Ken Wallace, who would have a long association with the team, joined in the middle of 1953, and left after transitioning into the Cougar in March 1956. Wallace, having flown numerous types of single-engine fighters, compared the Blue Angels' recently departed F9F-5s with the new F9F-8:

At that time, in the development of the swept-wing airplanes, they really had not solved the problem of what is known as the "Dutch Roll." The airplane was pretty sloppy about the vertical axis. They added a large fillet between the trailing edge of the wing and the fuselage on the -8, which served to dampen that out a little bit. Grumman also increased the size of the stall fences on the wing.

The F9F-8, and -8T shown here, had wet wings with fuel dump valves in the tips. Fuel dye was added to give color to the dumped fuel. *Cormier collection*

The -8, as opposed to the -5, was a flaperon airplane. That introduces a different control feel than you are accustomed to in an airplane that has ailerons on each wing. The worst feature of a flaperon airplane is the fact that there is a break-out force. If you want to make a turn, you initiate a movement with the stick. It takes some force to get the flaperon up into the slipstream. We finally, when we got to the F11F for instance, put both flaperons on the leader's airplane up just a few degrees, just enough to put the flaperons up into the air stream so that you did not have that force required to break it away from its position on the wing.

You just got pure control input.

The -8 was also a "flying tail" airplane, which was considerably different than the -5's conventional tail.

## Flying the Cougar in the Show

Team leader Cormier described the new routine used with the new Cougar:

We always prided ourselves on being precisely on time. You could set your clocks by us. If they said on the airshow schedule, "The Blue Angels will fly at 10:19," we would take off, go out feel the air, and we would plan it so that when the clock tick went to 10:19, we would be right over the field. We would brief this.

Our first pass would be a fly-past in formation just to show the people the Diamond Formation. In those days, when you could fly where you wanted to, I would stick it right on the ground. Everybody in the crowd would ask, "Where did these guys come from?" Then, we would go into our regular routine. The Diamond

Capt. Ed "Hoot" Rutty's F9F-8 BuNo. 138870 at Oakland, September 18, 1955. One of the US Air Force Thunderbirds has "zapped" Rutty's Cougar. Note the Thunderbirds sticker above the "y" in Navy. *William T. Larkins*

The team was in its first season with the Cougars when this photograph was taken. Cdr. Zeke Cormier's F9F-8 heads up the line of parked Blue Angel aircraft at Oakland, September 18, 1955. *William T. Larkins*

When the team transitioned into the F9F-8 Cougars, the public information officer traded in his TV-2 for the new Grumman swept-wing cat. F9F-8T BuNo. 142470 is seen at Oakland prior to the airshow. *William T. Larkins*

Roll would be the second maneuver and then we would do a loop and come back in echelon and do the Left Echelon Roll, Cuban Eight, Fleur de Lis, Tuck Under Break—airplanes come in in left echelon, and then come in and land.

The solo pilots would come by upside down between the Diamond Formation, and do opposing passes, and then opposing passes into vertical rolls. So there was something going on over the field at all times. The Diamond would go by, then the solos would go by, followed by the Diamond. Then we did a six-plane loop. Nello Pierozzi

always wanted to do a Line-Abreast Loop. I told him that was too hard. Now, when we go see today's Blue Angels, they always do the Line-Abreast Loop. He really rubs it in. Then, we would come in and land, and taxi back in formation.

The leader did not have as much cockpit work, consciously, as did the wingman or slot pilot. You do a lot of those things more by feel than by conscious effort. You feel the nose come up, and you automatically react. It is not a conscious act. Only when you are doing a specific maneuver is there a routine you go through. The

We thought it looked sensational, but it wasn't. We were dumping vaporized fuel on everyone. We then went back to the smoke oil system shortly thereafter. We talked the idea of the smoke oil system over with the crew chief in charge of maintenance, Bob Edgar, and asked how we could do this. He said, "Give me a couple of days, and I'll talk to my troops." He came back with the idea of running a copper pipe down the outside of the airplane to the tail pipe. Simple fix. No engineering, none of the other administration required. He just got it done.

The troops that work on the airplanes have never gotten the recognition they deserve. Those guys are absolute geniuses. In the squadrons, it would take two days to change an engine, our guys could do it overnight. They have people that are absolute miracle workers, the cream of the crop. They flew around in an old, beat-up airplane. They had to leave before we did and they would come home after we did. Never complaining. We had a DC-3 that belonged to the station. Our routine was I would get ahold of the guy in operations and tell him we are leaving for Seattle on Wednesday, so pump up your airplane. If he could get a four-engine job, fine; if we ended up with a twin, it would take forever to get our guys out there. [The team finally got a four-engine Douglas R5D-4 Skymaster assigned in late 1955.]

Left Echelon Roll was the hardest for the guys on the wing. It is an unnatural act. It is something you never do when you are out in the fleet. You never turn in to your wingman. It is just a no-no. We did it just to show that it could be done, I guess. It looks so smooth. To find out what it was like to be on the end of the thing, I'd go up and fly it. It is tough out there. You're going full cob, full off, full nose up, full nose down. There is that much action in the cockpit.

The F9F-8 had wet wings with dump valve in the tips. The team again added fuel dye and went back to dumping colored fuel. Said Cormier:

To celebrate their 10th anniversary year, the team hosted a reunion of past and present Blue Angels at NAS New York. The team flew its first airshow on foreign soil on September 5, in Toronto, Canada.

After the last show of the season, Cormier prepared to turn over the squadron to another distinguished aviator. "I got orders to go to a West Coast squadron," Cormier said, "and I turned the Blues over to Ed Holley. I went from the Blues to VA-113 flying the A-4 Skyhawk."

The F9F-8 was good for its time, but as the science of aerodynamics grew, aircraft more compatible with the Blue Angels' mission were brought on line. That next step in aircraft design was the Grumman F11F Tiger.

51

Long-nose Tigers on the ramp at Oakland on September 6, 1959.
Blue Angel No. 6 is BuNo. 141867.
The Tiger's paint scheme was designed by Lt. Bob
Rasmussen, a member of the 1957–59 teams.
*Harrison W. Rued*

# Chapter Five

# The Blue Angels Go Supersonic

The age of supersonic flight came to the Blue Angels at the end of 1957. Cdr. Ed Holley guided the team's transition into the new swept-wing fighter. The fuselage was designed around the "area-rule" principal resulting in a clean, and when viewed from above, Coke-bottle-shaped fuselage. The high-aspect-ratio wing, coupled with an afterburning Westinghouse J-65-W-18 engine developing 7,450 pounds thrust, was capable of speeds in excess of Mach 1. Before committing to the Tiger, the team evaluated the North American FJ Fury and the McDonnell Douglas A-4 Skyhawk. New skipper Ed Holley described the transition:

Blue Angels 1957 team; standing, left to right: Lt. Herb Hunter, 1st Lt. Tom Jefferson (USMC), and Lt. Mark Perrault. Kneeling: Lt. Lefty Schwartz, Lt. Bob Rasmussen, Cdr. Ed Holley (team leader), and Lt. Nello Pierozzi. *Ed Holley collection*

The team was flying F9F-8s when I got there. Zeke Cormier had apparently been to Grumman and flown the F11. He talked about fuel slosh being a problem, but I did not find that. The first big airshow I went to back in those days was the Oklahoma Airshow. I was just watching—I wasn't the leader, Cormier was. That's when I saw the Thunderbirds with the F-100s and the noise they put out. When I got back to Pensacola, I went down to talk to the chief of staff about considering an afterburner-equipped airplane. Staff agreed, and sent me to Grumman to reevaluate the F11F Tiger.

Nello Pierozzi went with me to Grumman, and we flew quite a bit up there, for maybe a week. Our objective was to find out if the F11F would work as a team airplane. We found that we could use it very well. Pierozzi had the most experience on the team, having been a wingman and a slot man. We tried the F11 on the wing and in the slot and did not find any problems. When we returned, we told staff that the F11F could meet the team's needs. Staff went to the Chief of Naval Operations, and then we got them.

Cdr. Ed Holley leads the team in their new F11F-1 Tigers in a roll over Pensacola Beach, Florida, home of the US Navy Blue Angels. *Ed Holley collection*

When asked about the criticism regarding the Tiger's engine/airframe combination, Holley responded:

It wasn't my choice of engines. The plane came with the J-65. I don't understand why they didn't use the J-57 engine. It would have been a much better engine for that airplane. Fortunately my teams did not lose any airplanes on cross-country flights because of the engine. We had problems with them throwing oil over the starboard side. My main objection to the airplane was that it was very short-legged. It was a stronger airplane than the F9F-8, but the burner was the main reason for going to it. The afterburner's noise was

a crowd-pleaser. The F11F was a sleeker looking airplane also.

During the same period, the faithful Lockheed TO Shooting Star, flown by the advance-man, was retired. A two-place F9F-8T Cougar was acquired to replace it.

A new paint scheme was designed for the Tiger by right wing and, later, slot pilot Lt. Bob Rasmussen. The old scheme had US Navy in block letters, where Rasmussen's scheme featured the words "Blue Angels" in script lettering; the team's logo was moved behind the name, and "US Navy" was smaller. An arrow was drawn down the belly, and stripes were added on each side of the canopy. This paint scheme has been carried through the Phantom, A-4 Skyhawk, and onto today's F/A-18 Hornets. The planes were delivered from Grumman with the Rasmussen-designed paint scheme.

## Flying Shows in the Tiger

The team flew its first show in the F11F-1 at Barin Field, near Pensacola, on March 23, 1957. The Tiger's power, as compared to the Cougar's, allowed the team to elongate the vertical maneuvers. "At first," said Holley, "we were trying to fly shows on the weekend in the F9F-8, and train during the week in the F11. We finally had to give that up and stick with one bird because the pulls and speeds were completely different. Once we moved into the F11, we just stuck with it. We did not have any problems. You just had to get used to it; it was a different bird."

Holley had a fighter pilot's philosophy when it came to the look of a Blue Angels airshow in the Tiger. He believed that the vertical maneuvers looked the best, the closer to the crowd the better. The F11's afterburner allowed him to do this. It gave him the power to keep the show within the confines of the airfield. Holley said, "One of the ways we did this was, after a roll, we snapped it into burner and pulled vertical. At 6,500 feet you are on your back again looking at the runway, preparing for your next maneuver."

Flying a high, tight, close-in show is a matter of practice. The more familiar the team becomes with a maneuver, the closer to perfection it can be flown. Does the show site have an effect on the team's performance? Holley said no, but there were show sites that did require additional attention:

I was most concerned with shows over water. When putting on a show beside a carrier, you have no reference to the water unless you can see the mast of the ship. It's easy on a field, you watch for telephone poles and things like that to give you depth perception. I always checked my altimeter first and then any ground references to know where I was at every second during a show. I'm looking at those instruments and whatever else I need to watch—primarily the g-meter. The wingmen are busy holding formation and are focused on my aircraft.

Depending on what maneuver I was in, that dictated my instrument scan. In a loop I watched the g-meter, because I wanted to make it nice and round, and the airspeed indicator because I did not want it to get too slow across the top. Then the altimeter and airspeed coming back down. You are not going to pop your speed brakes on the down side of a loop, or the other three in the formation will fly right through you.

The leader has total responsibility of the lives of all four Diamond pilots. It requires a lot of concentration. Everything is acknowledged. For instance, if I said Left Echelon Roll, each pilot acknowledges with his aircraft number. You only have a few seconds to work the whole show in around communications and watching the instruments.

Every maneuver the team performs has been scrutinized to ensure that it can be performed safely. There has never been an element of daredevil in the team's maneuvers. These are professional aviators flying well-rehearsed aerial routines. Although there is an exception to that rule:

The one maneuver you really can't practice is the Fleur de Lis. You are breaking up and rolling and you are coming together and rendezvousing on the backside of a loop. The leader has to keep power back so the other members can catch up.

The 1958 team standing, left to right: Lt. Herb Hunter, Lt. Jack Dewenter, Lt. Bob Rasmussen, Capt. Stoney Mayock, and Lt. John Damian. Seated: Cdr. Ed Holley, team leader. *Ed Holley collection*

Zeb Knot took over the team from Ed Holley in 1959. His team (pictured) left to right: LCdr. Jack Reavis, Capt. Stoney Mayock (USMC), Lt. Bob Rasmussen, LCdr. Zeb Knott (team leader), Lt. Herb Hunter, Lt. John Damian, LCdr. Jack Dewenter, and Lt. Mark Perrault. *Ed Holley collection*

Of course you have speed brakes if you get too far ahead of where you want to be. I did not find any of the maneuvers difficult. They are not difficult if you have the right pilots, and I did.

No matter how much the team practices together, no matter the skills of the pilot in the cockpit, a $2 part can always fail at the wrong time. The pilot's judgment can mean the difference between a fantastic performance and a canceled show. A stuck valve almost ended one show for Holley:

At the show in Oakland, California, I started it off with the Diamond Roll. I was venting fuel from my wing tips and could not get the

valve to shut off. So I'm siphoning fuel from my main cell. I really had to be watching that one because I was almost down to zero. We finally got the show over and I got on the ground with just enough fuel to taxi in.

If a $2 part can have an effect on the team's performance, how about personal items? Said Holley:

I always wore the same pair of gloves until I had to throw them away because of the feel on that stick. Same thing with my shoes. I always wore the same pair of shoes for flying shows because of the feedback I got from the rudders. I

Blue Angels logo with F11Fs in formation. *Ron Strong*

did not want anything to change. You want that feeling the same each time. When the fourth plane comes into the slot, he pushes your nose over requiring you to trim back to hold him in position. Then the wingmen are moving in and holding tight formation. It is a locked formation.

## Back-to-Back Pass Was a Show Stopper

The two solo pilots on the 1958 team, Lt. John Damian and LCdr. Jack Dewenter developed the back-to-back pass. Both planes pass down the show line in formation; one pilot flies straight and level and the other flies inverted. "We developed that maneuver and held it until the Andrews Air Force Base Airshow, because that's where we wanted to show it," Holley said. "Curtis LeMay was there, and my public-information officer was standing next to him. Reportedly, LeMay threw his cigar down and said, 'I don't believe this.'"

New short-nose F11F Tigers on the ramp at Oakland. The F11F featured an afterburning engine and had an aerial refueling probe in the nose. *Harrison W. Rued*

Side profile view of the Tiger. Note tail skid and nose refueling probe. *William T. Larkins*

## Training Site Moved

Holley went to El Centro his first year, 1957, for winter training. The next year he moved the team to Key West. He said, "I liked the idea of being closer to Pensacola. You got mail back and forth, and I did not like to keep the men that far away from home. It wasn't necessary. I thought Key West was great. Staff didn't care where you went, just so you were ready to go at show time."

## Adding New Team Members

Holley's team selected the new members as a group. Most of the Blue Angel candidates came to the team from the training command. The team would issue a memo stating their need for two new pilots each year. Usually somewhere between 20 and 30 pilots would apply, and after the team reviewed their flight records, those who made the "first cut" were invited to fly with the team. The selectees flew with each member of the team in the Diamond and flew each position in the formation. Holley described the selection process:

We would take them out and do vertical maneuvers, lots of rolls, and see how they could hold their position. They stay with the team for a week or two to find out if they are drunkards, or good speakers. Your life depends on this guy, and you are going to be out with the public. Airshows are show business. You are going to be on TV, interviewed by reporters, fly celebrities, news media, and local politicians.

After hosting each pilot we had invited to fly, the team would sit down in the ready room and review each flight and then decide which person we wanted to ask to join the team. Once the decision was made, we would call the Bureau of Personnel and request that the order be cut. It was pretty much a team selection.

## Battling the Bureaucracy

Holley described dealing with bureaucracy and the rest of the Navy:

Back in our time, the rest of the Navy was not enthusiastic about the team. They considered us showmen and never realized how hard we worked. We were on the job seven days a week and only got about two weeks off a year. We were flying shows until the first of November. Then we took a couple of weeks off, and then began our winter training again. The team was back on the road again in February. Then it is every weekend, and we were flying two shows, Saturday and Sunday in every case. Plus we flew practice shows during the week.

When we would come out to the West Coast, we would usually try to start our shows down south and move all the way up to Seattle instead of running back and forth from Pensacola. Then I had my support crew to consider. If we were going to be on the West Coast for two weeks, we would switch support crews during the middle of it. Send the R5D back with the people you have and bring out a new crew.

It was also tough to get parts. The yaw damper is a part that the No. 4 guy needed because his vertical stabilizer was in my jet-stream most of the time. His tail was always black. We were at Moffett Field, and we had a yaw damper go out. There was an F11F squadron there, and I went over and asked the skipper if I could get a yaw damper and I'd replace it. He did not want any part of it. One gets to the point where you've got to have it. So you go to the phone and call your boss in Pensacola. He calls Washington; they call out here and tell the skipper to give me the part. That should not happen. We are all wearing the same uniform. We've all got a job to do, and you feel that you want to do the best that you can. There just wasn't that support for the team then.

## Holley's final thoughts:

After a show you would get out of the plane wringing wet, and the crowd would give you a standing ovation. That makes you feel that you've done a good job. I enjoyed the satisfaction of doing a good show and reading the good reviews in the newspapers.

It was a real close team. We never had any problems. I did not want any accidents and did not have any. [The only accident that occurred during Holley's watch was the loss of Nick

Rare and unusual photo of all Blue Angel aircraft types on board the USS *Kearsarge* (CVA-33). From left, Grumman F8F Bearcat, Grumman F9F-5 Panther, Grumman F9F-8 Cougar, and Grumman F11F Tiger. *John M. Campbell collection*

Glasgow, who was slated to relieve Holley.] I had been out with him in the morning in the F9F-8T to show him how to do reversals—the speed, the altitude, the g's. He was an F11 pilot and former squadron commander. I told him when he came to us, "Use 1,000 feet as your base instead of zero." Sadly, he did not do that. That afternoon he came down the backside of a reversal and got too low. He kept pulling back and pulling back until he finally mushed into the sand dunes."

## Knott Leads Team During Golden Anniversary of Naval Aviation

Cdr. Zeb Knott took over from Ed Holley after Nick Glasgow's death. Knott was designated officer in charge on December 8, 1959. Under Knott, the team made two foreign appearances: Bermuda in spring 1959 and at the Canadian Exhibition, Toronto, Canada, in fall 1960. The Golden Anniversary of Naval Aviation was celebrated in 1961. The Blue Angels were Naval Aviation's ambassadors, flying in 74 shows for more than 5 million spectators. During the year-long festivities, the team flew for the dedication of NAS Lemoore, California, and in tribute to the "birthplace of Naval Aviation," NAS North Island, San Diego. Knott turned over command of the team to LCdr. Ken Wallace in the aerial change of command ceremony on January 16, 1962.

Left
Tiger Diamond formation salutes the Statue of
Liberty in New York harbor. *Cormier collection*

Left below
Mt. Rushmore's residents get an up-close view of the
supersonic cats flown by the Blue Angels. *Cormier collection*

## Ken Wallace Returns as Team Leader

Said Wallace:

> I came back in July 1961. The F11F was a
> more refined airplane than the F9F-8 and a lot
> sleeker and certainly more aesthetically pleasing
> from the standpoint of an airshow airplane. The
> F11F retained the characteristics of being a
> swept-wing airplane with a flying tail. It did have
> an afterburner that we used on a good number
> of maneuvers. We also used the afterburner
> extensively at high-density altitude shows. You
> needed that extra thrust to get around in some
> of the maneuvers at high and hot airshows.
> Without the afterburner, the F11F did not jump
> around with a great deal of alacrity.

As the team leader in 1962, Wallace introduced a number of new maneuvers. One of the
first was the Farvel. The maneuver calls for the
Diamond Formation with only the leader inverted. How did the team come up with the name
"Farvel?" Wallace explained: "There was a commercial for Nestle's chocolate on TV at that time,
and a dog in the commercial was named Farvel.
On the spur of the moment I decided to call that
maneuver the Farvel. No better reason than that."

The Diamond Landing (four planes) and
Delta Landing (six planes) were also introduced.
A runway 150 feet wide could accommodate the
Delta Landing, and on narrower, 100-feet-wide
runways, the Diamond Landing was performed.
"About the biggest thing you had to be concerned with," Wallace said, "was if somebody got
a little foot heavy and blew a tire. If that happened you just had to spread out to give him
room to decelerate. We always considered it as
safe as all of the other maneuvers we were
doing." The six-plane Delta Landing calls for the
trailing members of the formation to land first,
followed by the two wingmen immediately after
that, and then the leader.

Tigers in right echelon trailing smoke and venting
fuel. *Cormier collection*

The Dirty Roll on Takeoff was a maneuver
Wallace had done in years past flying the A-4.
"When we were first getting the A-4 in the
fleet," he said, "I used to go around and
demonstrate the airplane to squadrons that
were supposed to get it. Those confidence
maneuvers, such as the Dirty Roll on Takeoff,
were some of the things I did. We decided to
do it in the F11."

Tigers perfectly aligned on the NAS Pt. Mugu ramp, March 1963. *Ron Strong*

At the beginning of 1961 the team had trained at Key West. For the 1962–63 practice session, Key West had gotten crowded with aircraft for the Cuban Missile Crisis. "There were just too many airplanes," Wallace said. "I looked around and we went to Litchfield Park, Arizona. That was really a nice training site for us because we were able to get a desert practice area. We had a couple of markers built and bulldozed a simulated runway. At this time we were essentially the only activity at Litchfield Park. They were about to close the field down, and I was able to get the field held open for us for a couple of years."

During the 1963 season, Wallace's team flew their 1,000th show, at NAS Lemoore, California. "Lemoore, for being out there in the middle of nowhere, always drew fantastic crowds," Wallace said. "For the 1,000th show, I

Above and opposite
Two views of the "Farvel" maneuver introduced by Ken Wallace's 1962 team. The wing and slot pilots fly right side up while the leader hangs upside down in his seat belt. Note the arrow on the bottom of the Tiger's fuselage. *Cormier collection*

think they put enough hype into it that they had record crowds. Lemoore is a good airshow site. It is fairly well isolated—no high-tension lines, sparse population."

## Aumack Takes the Team Abroad

Ken Wallace turned over the duties of officer in charge to Cmdr. Bob Aumack on January 3, 1964. During his second year in command, Aumack led the team on its first European tour. Departing Andrews Air Force Base, Maryland, on June 6, 1965, the Blue Angels flew the North Atlantic route to Europe. The tour lasted 32 days and included airshow per-

The 1962 team, from the left: Lt. Dick Langford, left wing; Lt. Dan MacIntyre, solo; LCdr. Ken Wallace, team leader; Lt. George Neale, slot pilot; Lt. Doug McCaughey, right wing; and Lt. Lew Chatham, solo. *Cormier collection*

formances at Le Bourget Airport (Paris) and Vichy, France; Helsinki, Finland; Copenhagen, Denmark; Arnheim, The Netherlands; Yeovilton, England; and en route back to the United States, at Keflavik, Iceland. For leading the team through an outstanding season, Aumack was awarded the Distinguished Flying Cross, while the other members of the team were presented with Air Medals.

LCdr. Dick Oliver was tragically killed in September 1966 when he failed to recover from a maneuver while flying at Toronto over Lake Ontario.

### Bill Wheat Leads the Last of the Tigers

Aumack was relieved by LCdr. Bill Wheat on January 10, 1967. Wheat flew the team out to El Centro for winter training. Shortly after their arrival on the west coast, on February 17,

Lt. Frank Gallagher was killed during a practice session when he was unable to recover from a maneuver. Gallagher's replacement, Capt. Ron Thompson, USMC, was also lost during a training session only two weeks later.

After putting the twin tragedies behind them, Wheat got the show on the road. On May 12, 1967, Wheat led the team to Andrews Air Force Base to head overseas for the second time. Wheat recalled the trans-Atlantic journey:

The team went to Paris to the International Air Salon. We did a transatlantic flight from Nova Scotia, down to the Azores, then over to Rota, Spain, and from there to Naples, Italy. We were in-flight refueled from Air Force KC-135s three times to get all the way to Naples. From Naples, we went to Aviano, Italy; then to Tunis-Carthage, Tunisia; then on to Paris. Later, we

The Tiger team was supported by Douglas R5D-3, BuNo. 50868. *Harrison W. Rued*

Spotting the No. 2 Tiger, May 1967, Santa Rosa. *Harrison W. Rued*

Nearing the end of their career, the Blue Angel Tigers line the ramp at Santa Rosa, California, May 1967. The Tiger would be phased out in favor of the McDonnell Douglas F-4 Phantom II at the end of the 1968 season. *Harrison W. Rued*

flew another show at an air base north of Naples before retracing our steps back home.

Flying overseas was a real challenge. Getting there was the first, and performing with four other demonstration teams was the second. The French team, the Italian team, the Thunderbirds, and [Britain's] Red Arrows all flew at the show. It was nice to fly with that group of friends that were in the same business from different coun-

tries. The camaraderie of the teams was felt and was really nice.

In early 1968, the Douglas R5D Skymaster support plane was transferred out of the squadron and replaced with a Lockheed C-121J Constellation. Later that season, Lt. Mary

How did the Farvel maneuver get its name? Team leader Ken Wallace said, "There was a commercial for Nestle's chocolate on TV at the time [1962], and a dog in the commercial was named 'Farvel.' On the spur of the moment, I decided to call that maneuver the 'Farvel.' No better reason than that." *Piccianni via John M. Campbell*

Right
F11F knife-edge pass venting red and blue dyed fuel. *Piccianni via John M. Campbell*

Russell reported aboard as the assistant public-affairs officer. Russell was the first woman on the team and served through the 1970 season.

Near the end of the season, the decision was made to transition the team from the faithful Grumman Tiger to the McDonnell Douglas F-4 Phantom II. Grumman aircraft had served the team well for 21 years.

Blue Angel Phantoms in the Diamond formation, February 1969.
*McDonnell Douglas*

# Chapter Six

# Phantoms: Raw Power, Tragic Team Member

Grumman's Tiger had served the team well. It was no longer being built and would soon become hard to support materially. Aeronautical engineering had made giant leaps between the time the F11F was designed and the Navy accepted its first McDonnell Douglas F-4J Phantom II. Team leader Bill Wheat described how the Phantom's extra power changed the routines:

I thought the F11F was a nice airplane to fly. It was under-powered in the sense that you had to fly away from the show site and then dive back down to get the airspeed you needed for some of the overhead maneuvers. There was time lost in the airshow because of that, and lags between the maneuvers of the Diamond and the solos. With the Phantom, we were able to fly all of the maneuvers in less time. We had a 22-minute airshow as the norm in the F11, and in the Phantom we could do the same number of maneuvers and the same sequence of maneuvers, in only 18 minutes. It would have knocked four minutes off the show schedule if we had stayed with the same maneuvers all because of the power the Phantom had to get back in front of the crowd. We were able to add additional maneuvers to the show and give the crowd another four minutes of airplanes, flying in front of them, in the same 22-minute airshow.

It was a very powerful airplane and very stable in the sense that it flew like an airplane should. That's the best compliment you can pay any piece of equipment. It was—I don't want to say forgiving—but powerful in the sense that you could get the power you needed to catch up with the other people in the flight. Power that might not have been available in the F11.

Once the team learned to deal with the Phantom's proximity effect, Wheat said they flew some extremely tight formations, but added: "We never flew a perfect airshow though. You never want to say you have done that. We flew some good ones, and we flew some that we were proud of as a group, but they never were prefect." Can you be more humble than that?

## Acquiring the Phantom

The Vietnam War was on, and available aircraft types for the Blue Angels to transition to were limited. The team needed a new airplane, but had not decided on what type. Wheat had considered the Vought F-8 Crusader, but Vought going out of the aircraft business just as the F11 production line was shutting down. Both aircraft were going to be hard to support very shortly. There were no F-8s available because

Blue Angel Phantom Dirty Diamond Pass, March 1968. Note that the under fuselage arrow has been carried onto the Phantom. *McDonnell Douglas*

of the involvement in Vietnam, and all of the McDonnell Douglas A-4s were required to meet the fleet's commitments.

"The way we got the F-4 was that we had heard that the Air Force was going to get them," said Wheat. He called his commanding officer, who called Washington. Wheat's argument was that the Phantom was designed for the Navy, and the Navy was the first to deploy the Phantom, so it was not fair that the Air Force's demonstration team would get the Phantom first.

Washington agreed to look into it. They found six F-4s out at NAS Oceana, Virginia, that were being used for carrier qualifications. "We called them 'lead nose F-4Js,'" Wheat said, "mean-

ing they had ballast in the nose rather than guns and equipment. They just used them to go out to the ship and carrier-qualify with them." Washington said those six aircraft might be available, and Wheat replied, "That's what we need."

Shortly thereafter, the Phantoms at Oceana were identified as being available. The Navy said those airplanes were not needed by the services because they were in excess of the normal need. All other Phantoms had been committed to operations in Vietnam. The "lead nose" Phantoms could not be reworked into fleet configuration—Wheat got lucky when those six were found. Transfer orders were cut, and Wheat's Oceana Phantoms were sent to

One solo right side up, one solo inverted trailing smoke, February 1969. *McDonnell Douglas*

McDonnell Douglas' St. Louis, Missouri, factory to be readied for use by the Blue Angels. Wheat recalled:

McDonnell Douglas had to paint the planes and put certain "feel" systems in for us. They had a sophisticated system of feel, and you would end up flying through a zero [or neutral] position of feel at some point. We had it changed over to a spring-and-bob-weight system that gave us 14 pounds of pressure at all times when we flew it with full nose down trim. You never want to have a neutral feel on the stick because it would be too hard to fly formation.

The afterburner was modulated in that you could modulate the burner from about 92 per-cent all the way up to 100 percent. What I did was I put a metal block in front of the afterburner area where I could stop the throttle in order to keep from outrunning the other planes in the formation. [Depending on a plane's position in the formation, they each accelerate slightly differently, and they needed the extra power to stay with the leader.] I limited my ability to go into 100 percent in afterburner so they had a few percent to play with and stay in formation. They worked their own throttle to accomplish their need for power, and I gave them the percentages to stay there by not going to full power.

One member of the team, Lt. Steve Shoemaker, had flown Phantoms before. The

The Phantom was a crowd favorite. To this day, videos of the team flying the F-4 are still popular sellers. Is there a better way to travel cross-country? In formation, inverted. *McDonnell Douglas*

Team Leader Bill Wheat taxies No. 1 in after a fantastic performance at NAS Moffett Field, California, on August 9, 1969. *Wayne McPherson Gomes*

team flew down to Key West for a day's orientation and flying in the F-4J.

"The team was briefed on safety procedures and power settings," Wheat said of the orientation. "Then we got in six of them and flew them around." The orientation went smoothly, and the team looked forward to transitioning into the new fighter.

"I picked up the first F-4 on December 23 at McDonnell Douglas in St. Louis and flew it back to Sherman Field."

## Phantom Airshows

Wheat described the early airshows in the Phantom:

Some of the big show sites that were exciting to fly at were Warner-Robbins Air Force Base, Georgia, for example. The width of the runway was over 300 feet there. In the Phantom, we were able to land six airplanes at one time. The best we could do at any other field was four airplanes fly-

ing in a Diamond to touchdown. At this field we could put the two solos on the side [of the Diamond] and fly the whole formation to landing. It is quite impressive to see six airplanes coming down at one time. The back row lands, then the second row lands, then the leader.

Every show site had its challenges and the benefits of the locals enjoying our performances and us enjoying their cities. Each host city extended their best hospitality to us. We flew in Alaska and that was kind of exciting, too. To fly up over that beautiful and snowy terrain and see the wild animals down below as we were transgressing the area between the show sites.

One of the most impressive maneuvers, and one that highlighted the Phantom's raw power, was the Dirty Loop on takeoff. Wheat described it: "We could just leave the gear and flaps down and go right up over the top after takeoff."

In August 1969, the Phantom demonstrated its ability to exceed the speed of sound at

Capt. Vince Donile in Blue Angel No. 2 leads the rest of the formation out for their performance at NAS Moffett Field, August 9, 1969. *William T. Larkins*

## Kelowna, British Columbia. Wheat described the embarrassing consequences of the event:

We were practicing over the waterfront area. There are mountains on either side and a straight flight line above the waterfront and the center of town. We were practicing the crossing maneuver where we broke apart at altitude, and we came down and crossed in front of the crowd from four different directions. Ernie Christensen was flying No. 3 and Vince Donile was flying No. 2. When Christensen saw that Donile was going to be late for the crossover, he told him to hustle. When he told him that, Donile put it into burner and didn't quite take it out in time, and he broke the sound barrier right at the crossing. He made the cross, but we knocked all of the windows out for eight city blocks.

The mayor's office sat right on the waterfront looking out on a nice beautiful park and water. We had been in his office earlier in the day to receive a key to the city, and I'm sorry to say his whole 8-foot by 10-foot glass window was knocked out.

They had a parade scheduled for the next day, and they had to cancel that. All the windows were boarded up when we drove downtown. There were signs on the boarded-

Bill Wheat leads the Diamond formation takeoff at NAS Moffett Field, on August 9, 1969. The large structure near the P-3s is one of three airship hangars at the air station. *William T. Larkins*

up windows saying, "Yankee Go Home." So I got the city fathers together that night and told them it was an error, a mistake that we would not make again if they would please let us fly. I told them we would fly very safe and sane—a good airshow. Thankfully, they said OK. We flew a beautiful airshow for them the next day. It was rather embarrassing, to say the least.

## Making Maintenance's Life Easier

The Phantom was a very maintenance-intensive aircraft. It required a large support staff and, by nature, being a larger and more sophisticated aircraft than its predecessor, more spare parts. The Constellation was unable to meet the team's increased demands, and the team retired it on December 21, 1970. The plane was placed into Davis-Monthan Air Force Base, Tucson, Arizona, and was eventually scrapped. Wheat described why the Connie was replaced and how they acquired a C-130:

> The Constellation was an airplane that we had acquired some two to three years before. The best thing I think I did for the team was to insist that they replace the Connie with the C-130. The Navy said they had no C-130s because they were all involved in special operations, gunships, and that type of thing. The Navy said, "We just don't have any." I informed them the Marine Corps has a number of C-130s. They looked into it, and they came up with a C-130 for the team—after I left, and it has been with them ever since.
>
> The Connie was horrible. We had to have a forklift everywhere we went. That was the only way to get things into the Connie's cargo bay. All the tools, equipment, spare engines. It really took some effort on the part of the maintenance team to do that. I marveled at how they could work with such a handicap. It was really something.

The team has been supported by the US Marine Corps C-130s for the last 26 years, and will probably have C-130 aircraft for the foreseeable future. The C-130 Hercules offers a roll-on, roll-off cargo bay and had the capability to in-flight refuel the Blue Angels on long cross-country flights.

Six Phantoms pass in review. *William T. Larkins*

Phantoms were the first team aircraft equipped with a drag chute. *William T. Larkins*

## World Events, Accidents Spell End Of Phantom Era

"I turned the team over to Harley Hall," Wheat said. "He was an F-4 pilot out of one of the operating squadrons, and he had a lot of good F-4 time when he came to the team." The Phantom team under Hall introduced the Line-Abreast Loop—a maneuver that Nello Pierozzi wanted to do in the mid-1950s, and the Inverted Fleur de Lis. The aircraft's power gave the solos the opportunity to introduce Opposing Dirty Rolls on Takeoff.

Cmdr. Harley Hall took the Blue Angels to the Far East in 1971. The Phantoms required two in-flight refuelings, one by the team's C-130 and a second by an Air Force KC-135, en route to Hawaii. The team launched from (October 13) and recovered at (November 29) NAS Miramar, San Diego, California. During their 47 days abroad, they performed for crowds in Guam, the Philippines, Taiwan, Korea, and Honolulu.

LCdr. Don Bently became the team's fourteenth officer in charge on January 8, 1972. After the team had arrived at NAS El Centro for winter training, Lt. Larry Watters was killed while flying alone. His aircraft was last seen flying inverted, before he struck the ground. After a period of mourning, the team once again moved forward. Despite the setback suffered early in the year, the team had a successful season.

The darkest year in Blue Angels history came in 1973. In the early weeks of the year, at an El Centro training session, three of the Diamond formation aircraft were involved in a mid-air collision. After colliding, Bently, LCdr. Marlin Witta, and Marine Capt. John Fogg ejected, team leader Bently injuring his back. Bently's injuries were severe enough that he was unable to finish his term as team leader. LCdr. Skip Umstead was called upon to lead the team in Bently's place.

Umstead had flown as the second solo pilot during the 1970 season, and moved up to lead

The Lockheed C-121 Constellation joined the team in 1968. The cargo bay was over 10 feet off the ground and required that a forklift be on hand at each show site. Note the ladder extending from the cargo bay, between the number one and two engines, and the forklift parked behind the main landing gear. The Connie was retired on December 21, 1970. Team leader Bill Wheat said of the Constellation, "The best thing I think I did for the team was to insist that they replace the Connie with the C-130." *William T. Larkins*

solo for '71 and '72. On May 23, Umstead led the team over the Atlantic on a European tour. The Blue Angels performed at the Paris International Airshow and in Spain, Iran, Turkey, and Italy. Early in July, the team was back in the United States and flew an outstanding show in the Bahamas for England's Prince Charles. Days later, Lt. Steve Lambert was forced to eject from his crippled Phantom. Lambert survived uninjured, but the aircraft was a total loss.

The lowest point for the team came on July 26, 1973, at NAS Lakehurst, New Jersey. Upon arrival at NAS Lakehurst, Umstead's aircraft and that of Marine Capt. Mike Murphy collided in the air. Riding with Umstead was PO1C Gerald Harvey, while PO1C Ronald Thomas was in the back seat of Murphy's Phantom. Both petty officers were engine specialists on the maintenance team. Harvey was able to eject from the F-4, but Umstead, Murphy, and Thomas rode the fighters to their deaths.

After the accident, the Blue Angels' season was canceled. The country was in the grip of the fuel crisis. Long lines formed at gas stations around the country. The Navy worried about the public's perception of a flight demonstration team that flew gas-guzzling, expensive-to-maintain multi-role fighters as exhibition aircraft. This, combined with the abbreviated season and loss of aircraft and lives spelled the end of the Phantom era.

After the Phantom accidents, the team was rebuilt
with solid maneuvers and airmanship. Here the
Blue Angels execute a tight formation pass at Reno.
*Karen B. Haack*

# Chapter Seven

# Rebuilding the Team with "Good Solid Airmanship and Good Solid Maneuvers"

After the tragic 1973 season, the Blue Angels were floundering. Ken Wallace, 1954–55 slot pilot and 1961–63 team leader, was called upon to guide the team through rough waters. Wallace was serving in the office of the Chief of Naval Operations as his tactical-air-plans officer. Wallace said:

> Because of my past association with the Blue Angels, whenever anything that concerned them came up, I was rung in on it in some way. When we changed leaders [after Bently's accident], there was a lot of talk about putting a lieutenant commander in there. I was all for that. I knew Skip Umstead, and I knew his capabilities. I strongly urged them to put him in there. Later, he was involved in the accident at Lakehurst in which he was killed.
>
> In the view of the Secretary of the Navy that was

The TA-4J flown by the team's public affairs officer. *John M. Campbell collection*

almost the straw that broke the camel's back. He was not fully supportive of keeping the team. Adm. Zumwalt, who was the Chief of Naval Operations and not an aviator, was very much insistent on keeping the team in business. So he and I went to chat with the Secretary of the Navy. The Secretary agreed to keep it in business, but we had to change airplanes. He would not let us continue with the F-4s—partially due to the crashes, and at this point we were in the fuel crunch of the mid 1970s. The F-4 is not an economical airplane on fuel and it is a heavy maintenance airplane. It was just a little bit too visible for the times.

## Selecting A New Aircraft

Given the job of program manager for the Blue Angels, Wallace had his work cut out for him. Drawing on his previous experience with the team, he would implement many far-reaching changes. "I started casting about for a different airplane. The airplane that I really wanted was the F-14," he said. "I did not want an F-14 with all the weapons control systems in it, that was wasteful." After proposing his

Flying past vertical, the team heads into a loop.
*McDonnell Douglas*

idea to Grumman, they decided that it would cost more to make an airplane without the systems than it would with them. Cost became the determining factor, and the F-14 idea went by the wayside.

For Wallace, the A-7 was the next logical choice. He said:

> There simply was not enough airplanes in the pipeline to let us have them. The fleet needed the airplane desperately and could not divert seven aircraft for our use. I went down to Chance

Vought and flew the airplane, and it certainly would have been quite suitable.

Although it had been looked at by a number of team leaders in the past, Wallace once again considered McDonnell Douglas' A-4 Skyhawk:

> The A-4 was about the only fleet airplane left that was anywhere near usable by the team. It just so happened that while we were doing this search for airplanes, a couple of squadrons were coming back from Vietnam and were being decommissioned. They had the A-4F, which was the latest model at that time. They also had the latest engine, the P-408. It had more thrust than any of the previous engines the A-4 had used.
>
> We got together with the engineers at McDonnell Douglas and with some of the people at Naval Air Systems Command. We needed some changes to the control system. We needed more nose-down force. Traditionally, the Blue Angels fly the airplane, regardless of the model, with full down-nose trim. It gives us, in some cases, 40 pounds of nose-down stick force. We want that nose-down force so we've got something we are putting pressure against all the time. Plus, in rough air it tends to make you bounce away from the formation rather than up into the airplanes ahead of you. By bracing our right forearms on our leg or knee, it provides a very stable or firm base to control the airplane with the stick. By just flexing your wrist a little bit, rather than having large-magnitude arm movements, you get your control that way. The engineers at McDonnell Douglas came up with a bungee-cord arrangement that modified the bell crank assemblies in the airplane, thus providing the nose-down force.
>
> We also bolted up the leading-edge slats. The A-4, in its normal configuration, has aerodynamic slats on the leading edges of the wings. They are actuated by aerodynamic force and are used in heavy g loads or accelerations. They increase the camber of the wing so that you get more lift. The problem with those aerodynamic slats is that, depending on the condition of flight, if you're not exactly in balanced flight or if you are in a turn, one slat may not come out and the other may fully deploy. It really depends on the air loads. If they come out asymmetrically, they can pop you right on your

Over the top of the Diamond Roll. *McDonnell Douglas*

back faster than you can think about it. We determined that by bolting them up we would not add to the landing speed of the airplane by any significant amount.

We took the guns out, some armor plating, added a drag chute for operations from shorter airports, and added weight to the nose for balance. The overall weight reduction was significant. We ended up with an airplane that weighed 11,300 pounds [dry] and we had an engine that produced 11,400 pounds thrust. When you got down to a light fuel load, you could do some pretty cute tricks with that little airplane. The roll rate would certainly not spin your head, but it was more than enough for what we wanted to do in the airshow.

## Making the Team "A Real Squadron"

While Wallace was in the process of selecting an aircraft and making the necessary modifications, he was busy making other changes:

A little help from a big friend. Fitted with long-range drop tanks, the team formates with an Air Force KC-10 aerial-refueling aircraft during a long over-water flight. *McDonnell Douglas*

Cdr. Tony Less leads the 1975 team in salute to the USS *Lexington* (CVT-16) in the gulf waters off NAS Pensacola. *McDonnell Douglas*

If an aviator came to the Blue Angels as a commander and spent two years there, because of the timing of things, most likely he was also at the point in his career when he was going to be selected for squadron command. If his contemporaries were getting their squadrons, and he was down here as head of the Blue Angels, it was penalizing him. That was one of the prime reasons for making it a squadron, so that he would be able to count it as having a squadron command for his tour with the Blues.

It also made the Blue Angels eligible for the full complement of squadron personnel. I did not choose to go that route. I wanted to keep it very austere and very small. Instead of the full A-4 complement of enlisted personnel, we took

only 63. That is less than half what the normal squadron would get. We only took seven A-4Fs, plus the TA-4, when a squadron complement would have been 12. What it also did was to open up the supply channels to us a little bit. We no longer had to go to several sources to get parts.

We could have had a lot more ground-support officers, but I wanted to keep that at a minimum also. I kept the people who were already on board in those billets.

They had already made a selection for the leader. I took the people who were left on the team, there were only a couple of them, and I selected the remainder. Most of the people on the team had never flown the A-4 before, so we were busy training those people. The new leader

The US Marine Corps provides a C-130 and crew in support of the Blue Angels. The C-130 gets into the act with a late evening jet-assisted takeoff (JATO). *John M. Campbell collection*

[Cdr. Tony Less] was deployed at the time. When he came on board, I went out and flew with him.

The Blue Angels held their commissioning ceremony on December 10, 1973, at Pensacola. VAdm. Jerry Miller, former Sixth Fleet commander, was the guest speaker, and McDonnell Douglas presented the squadron with a painting for its ready room. At the commissioning ceremonies, only one aircraft had been painted into the team's colors, the two-seat TA-4J. This plane served as the backdrop for the ceremony.

After officially becoming a squadron, the team continued to train for an additional four weeks at Pensacola. They then moved to their winter home at El Centro for a full training cycle. Ken Wallace stayed on board until August 1974. Once

An A-4 Diamond pass, perfect for photographers, at the National Championship Air Races, Reno, Nevada, September 1982. *Karen B. Haack*

Team leader Dave Carroll taxies Blue Angel No. 1 past the crowd at Reno. *Karen B. Haack*

everyone was trained and on the road, he felt things were going well: "I considered that I had done what I set out to do, so I moved on." Wallace retired from the Navy after successfully guiding the Blue Angels through their lowest point.

## Getting the House in Order

Cmdr. Tony Less was the Blue Angels' first commander to have had a previous squadron command. He implemented additional changes to the squadron while in training. A flight surgeon was added, said Less:

> ... who was able to be a confidant of the commanding officer and respond to personality issues and changes. I think that was extremely beneficial. My relationship with the flight surgeon was good, and his was good with the rest of the team members too. But by the same token, he was able to put his finger on any little problems that might be coming up. When you are flying that close together, operating that close together, and living that close together for so long a period in the team environment, you need a guy like that.

As the Diamond pilots lift off into the late afternoon sun, No. 4 slides into the slot. *Karen B. Haack*

Prior to the team becoming a squadron, paperwork was, as always, a nightmare. Some years, the team had an administration officer and some years they did not. The officer, in charge spent many hours shuffling routine paperwork that could have been handled by a subordinate officer. Under the squadron, Less was able to have a permanent administration officer assigned.

Another bridge to cross dealt with morale and camaraderie. Before the team became a squadron, everyone except for the pilots, narrator, and public-affairs officer were excluded from being a Blue Angel. "When we went to a squadron," Less said, "we made sure that everyone understood that they were all Blue Angels. It added to the cohesiveness of the group. Prior to 1973, the support personnel considered themselves just support personnel. That was a major flaw that we had to overcome."

## Skyhawks Return to the Air, Cautiously

Less put the squadron through its paces at El Centro, flying twice a day, seven days a week, for two months. While training and rebuilding the squadron, the lessons learned by earlier teams were never far from this squadron's mind. Said Less:

> We realized that if we had an accident, it would probably mean the demise of the organization, so we approached the show season in a mode wherein we were certainly going to be aggressive, to practice perfection, but we were going to do basic maneuvers. I think the first year we worked ourselves into a routine that the airplane was capable of, and then the following years more maneuvers got put in.

Using caution as his guide, Less kept the Farvel out of the show until mid-1974. He also kept the solos from doing opposing rolls, where both aircraft roll toward each other. He continued:

Dave Carroll deploys his drag chute on Reno's short runway. *Karen B. Haack*

After we had gotten through the first year with no accidents, and we felt confident with the airplane and ourselves, we began to add a few more maneuvers. We went to a five-plane Fleur de Lis and a five-plane Line-Abreast Loop. We just started making things a little more aggressive. We tried to get maneuvers back a little bit tighter, reversals a little bit tighter. You can do that with a second-year team and a second-year boss as well. As K. C. Jones came on, some of the same team members were with him. They went to the Double Farvel, where the leader and the slot are inverted while the wingmen are right side up. They changed some of the solo maneuvers to where they were doing more outside stuff, such as negative-g push-outs.

I think our first year's philosophy was, "Lets get through this first year with good solid airmanship and good solid maneuvers." You are able to get a good tight show and have a maneuver in front of the crowd at all times; I think

that's what we did. Went at it with aggressiveness, but again, we minimized the risk factor. It continued to grow after that. We got through the first two years without losing anyone.

Thankfully, the rebuilding process and show seasons had been safe. Small incidents, that could have turned out for the worse had it not been for superior airmanship, did crop up now and then. Vance Parker was practicing at El Centro when one of his wings gave way. Parker had fuel in the wing and was doing vertical rolls. Less described the incident:

He was practicing full-aileron-deflection rolls and got the airplane rolling so fast that he popped some rivets in the wing while going straight up. The speed of that roll was such that it put fuel to the outer extension of the wing. The hydraulic pressure of the fuel split the wing apart because of the centrifugal force from that roll.

Splitting off into the Fleur de Lis. *Karen B. Haack*

Double Farvel—both the leader and slot are inverted.
*Ron Strong*

After that maneuver, his plane was leaking and his fuel gauge was going down. He put it back on deck OK, but we had to get a new wing for that airplane. We had never experienced this before, and clearly McDonnell Douglas never had either.

To prevent this from happening during an airshow, Less had to limit the solo pilots to three-quarter-stick-deflection rolls after the incident.

## Show Types Get Names

The team came equipped with three new tools for the 1974 show season. They had developed, or given names to, the "high" show, "low-rolling" show, and the "flat" show. Less described the conditions under which each type of show was flown:

Teams in the past had been doing that sort of thing; I just don't think they called it by those names. We decided that with the A-4 airplane, we were certainly able to do a straight flat show if the weather met VFR [Visual Flight Rules] standards [1,000-foot ceiling with 3-mile visibility underneath the cloud cover]. Then there were times when we would perform a rolling show. In the rolling show, we needed to have about 3,500 feet to do the rolls underneath the clouds. We topped out on the Delta Roll a little higher than the Diamond Roll. You could take a Diamond around just a little bit faster. With the six planes you wanted to make sure that you were not whipping too hard

Entering the Line-Abreast Loop. *Karen B. Haack*

Coming down the backside and rolling out of the Line-Abreast Loop. *Karen B. Haack*

Double Farvel. *Ron Strong*

The maneuvers the team performs are precise, timed, safe, and extensively practiced. *Ron Strong*

The A-4s line up at NAS Patuxent River, Maryland, September 1977. *John M. Campbell collection*

for those guys on the back corners. About 3,500 feet kept us from creeping into the clouds.

When there where clear skies with unlimited visibility, the team would fly their standard high show.

## Performance Highlights

The first performance for the public with the new A-4 Skyhawk was at Offutt Air Force Base, Nebraska, on May 18, 1974. Less had turned the squadron over to Cdr. K. C. "Casey" Jones on January 9, 1976. Jones would lead the team through the year-long Bicentennial celebrations. On July 4, the team performed for record crowds at NAS Willow Grove, Pennsylvania. The team also flew outside the United States for audiences at NAS Roosevelt Roads, Puerto Rico, and Abbotsford, Moose Jaw, and the city of Saskatchewan, Canada. While on the road, the team's winter home was renamed by the Navy. NAS El Centro became the National Parachute Test Range or NPTR El Centro.

Jones turned the squadron over to Cdr. Bill Newman in December 1977. Under Newman, the first enlisted female joined the squadron. Aviation Electronics Technician Penny Edwards became the first in a long line of women who have joined the ranks as Blue Angels technicians. While preparing for the last show of the 1978 season, Lt. Mike Curtin, opposing solo, was lost at NAS Miramar. Curtain was performing a high-speed, rolling pass down the flight line when he struck the runway. This tragic incident was the first loss of a Skyhawk aircrew.

## The End of the A-4 Era

On July 13, 1985, at the Niagara Falls Airport, two A-4s collided in mid-air during a performance. Two soloists, LCdr. Robert M. Gershon and Lt. Anthony P. Caputi had just completed a low opposing pass when they rolled inverted and pushed up into a Half Cuban Eight. The wing and fuselage of Gershon's aircraft struck the tail of

Caputi's. Caputi was able to eject, but Gershon perished, unable to get out of the stricken Skyhawk.

This unfortunate accident accelerated the examination of McDonnell Douglas' F/A-18 Hornet for use by the team. Navy officials had been considering the change for at least a month prior to the accident.

The team completed the 1985 show season, albeit with only one solo, and converted to the F/A-18 during the winter training session for the 1986 season.

Cmdr. Less summed up the Blue Angels' A-4 experience:

> The A-4 lasted for 13 years in the demonstration environment. In my estimation, it was the best airplane—I thought it looked great, and it was very maneuverable. You were able to keep the tops of your loops in the 6,500- to 6,800-foot range, reversals were tighter, and you could keep airplanes in front of the crowd consistently. The A-4 shows did not have gaps. It was a nice performing airplane.

Even the planes are precisely parked. *John M. Campbell collection*

A-4F tails at Reading, Pennsylvania, 1974. *Rick Alexander via Campbell collection*

View from the slot position, as the team rolls over the top.
*McDonnell Douglas*

# Chapter Eight

# The F/A-18 Hornet Years (1986 to Present)

The F/A-18 Hornet, now serving in more than 30 US Navy and Marine Corps squadrons, represented an entire change of philosophy for the Navy and the Marine Corps, the two US military services employing the front-line aircraft. No longer just fighters, the aircraft of today's military are more often referred to as "airborne weapons systems platforms." The change in thinking was a deliberate attempt to merge the two primary duties of today's Navy in one aircraft.

## Two Jobs, One Aircraft

The Navy needed carrier-based aircraft to do two jobs: interception of enemy aircraft entailing the engagement in advanced combat maneuvering (dogfighting) tactics and aircraft that could be used to carry out weapons delivery (bombing). The single-seat F/A-18 Hornet was designed, at the flip of a switch, to carry out either of these duties (there have even been cases where both capabilities have been called upon in a single mission).

## This Hornet is Painted Blue

On November 8, 1986, for the squadron's 40th anniversary, the Blue Angels received the keys to the McDonnell Douglas F/A-18 Hornet. The strike fighter, ironically, replaced two of the team's former aircraft: the F-4 Phantom II and the A-4F Skyhawk. The twin-tailed, stubby-winged Hornet comes equipped with two highly reliable F404-GE-400 low-bypass turbofan engines. The powerplants, made by General Electric, are capable of producing 32,000 pounds of thrust each.

Engine reliability is of particular concern for a demonstration team, especially when you take into account the close quarters they are flying during the Diamond and Delta formations. If one afterburner fails to light up at exactly the same time as the others the maneuver looks bad, at best, and the plane, at worst, could veer into one of the others.

Among some of the other outstanding features of the Hornet is the Hughes APG-65 radar—a powerful long-range detection system slimmed down to fit into the needle-like Hornet nose. The APG-65 can detect threats from both head-on and tail-on aspects. For use with the Blues, the aircraft's 20mm cannon was removed and replaced with a smoke system.

## High-Tech Hornet

The F/A-18, first flown in November 1978, introduced the world to the all-glass cockpit. Three

# Fighter Evolution: From Tiger to Hornet

The F/A-18 Hornet's genesis lay back in the F-5 Tiger II. In 1966, Northrop was looking to replace the single-engined F-5E. Company thinking intended it to be an air-superiority fighter able to achieve Mach 2 as an interceptor. In 1966, Northrop submitted a proposal for a new aircraft much like the F-5E with shoulder-mounted wings and slightly swept and shelf-like leading-edge root extensions (LERX).

The next year, Northrop made the LERX bigger, put the engine inlets behind the wing, and added trailing-edge fillets. The LERX was extended again in 1968, and the trailing-edge fillets were removed, but the biggest change was the twin tail. In 1969, the LERX was shaped, giving it a snake-like look. By the following year, the project was officially called P-530 but was unofficially dubbed "Cobra," with a refined fuselage, and the intakes had been cut back further.

Northrop's project eventually became a submission to an Air Force call for proposals for a Light Weight Fighter (LWF) as the P.600. On April 13, 1972, the Air Force awarded prototype contracts to two companies to build their design concepts: General Dynamics and its YF-16 entry, and the Northrop submission, now known as the YF-17. The YF-17 proved to have a maximum air speed of Mach 1.95, a service ceiling of more than 50,000 feet, and an angle of attack of 68 degrees. Nonetheless, on January 13, 1975, the Air Force chose the General Dynamics entry, which went on to become the highly successful F-16.

Soon, the Navy, at the direction of Congress, came looking to replace the shopworn F-4s and A-7s; the F-14's huge development and production costs were also making many nervous. Congress told the Navy to have a look at the derivatives from the LWF contest.

Northrop joined up with McDonnell Douglas, and the pair came up with the P-630, based somewhat on the smaller YF-17. The new entry would be required to carry AIM-7 Sparrow missiles and sophisticated radar for work as a dogfighter. For the attack mode, it would have to carry heavy external weapons stores. The Navy bird would have to have beefed-up gear to withstand the brutal punishment of landing and taking off of carriers, and, due to a carrier's storage limitations, it would need folding wings.

The project became known as the McDonnell Douglas Model 267. Finally, on May 2, 1975, Northrop and McDonnell Douglas (now named as prime contractor) were able to put a sold sign on their aircraft, and a contract for the building of development aircraft was issued. The aircraft was now referred to as the Naval Air Combat Fighter (NACF), and the intent was for one single-seat fighter to be made in two different variants: one for the fighter role (F-18) and one for the attack role (A-18).

The first development contract for the Hornet was made on January 22, 1976, calling for the two companies to build 11 aircraft, including two two-seat trainers. After early problems with wing loading, the wing area was increased. The first development model of what was to be known as the F/A-18 Hornet flew on November 18, 1978, the rest by 1980. In May 1980, VFA-125 at NAS Lemoore was the first to get their hands on the new jet for evaluation purposes (VFA-106 also performed an evaluative role with the F/A-18), but the first operational usage of the aircraft was officially by the Marine Corps squadron VMFA-314, the Black Knights, based at MCAS El Toro.

It wasn't until March 1983 that the first Navy squadron, VFA-25, began flying the aircraft, the same year that the Navy Reserves began flying the aircraft. VFA-113 became the first to take the aircraft to sea in 1985. In 1988, the orders for the aircraft stood at 1,168 aircraft for both the Navy and the Marine Corps.

There were 410 F/A-18A and TF-18A (later designated the F/A-18B). The first F/A-18C flew on September 2, 1987. The C model can carry up to six AIM-120 missiles, an AN/ALQ-165 radar jammer, and reconnaissance equipment. The C and D models (the two-seat version of the C) were later given all-weather and night-attack capabilities. Deliveries of the night-attack Hornet began in 1989.

CRT displays replaced the analog gauges (although, if you look hard enough, you will still find a couple tucked well away on the Hornet for backup. The force-multiplier aircraft (being both a fighter and an attack aircraft) has a service ceiling of 50,000 feet.

The airplane, in attack configuration, has an attack radius of 575 nautical miles. It can carry 11,000 pounds of fuel internally and another 5,000 if external tanks are used. Its maximum takeoff weight is 56,000 pounds when outfitted as a fighter escort. The aircraft's maximum speed is officially listed at Mach 1.8, but few Hornet drivers claim to have gotten the plane to that speed.

The Hornet is 56 feet long and 15.3 feet high. With missiles on the wing tip mounts, it

Blue Angel No. 3 at NAS Moffett Field awaits its driver. *Wayne McPherson Gomes*

has a wingspan of 40.4 feet. Its wing area is 400 square feet.

## They Like It Because It's Slow?

When you think of a fighter, you think naturally of high-speed action. The Hornet, in fact, excels in slow-speed handling—much handier from a fighter pilot's point of view. If you engage in a dog-fight at high speeds, it means you must make bigger turns. The slower your speed, the smaller your turn radius, which enables you to get inside of the faster guy and come in from behind him, always the preferred spot in aerial combat.

The F/A-18, as a Blue Angels aircraft, has had one of the best safety records. There was one winter training incident in 1990 when the No. 1 and No. 2 jets had a mid-air collision, but both pilots survived.

## New Plane, New Show

The F/A-18 Hornet, like its predecessors, provides for an entirely different Blue Angels show. Besides the sheer high-pitched noise of the two F404 turbofans, the aircraft has outstanding slow-speed handling capabilities. To demonstrate this, the high-alpha pass was a perfect choice for a new solo maneuver. In it, the airplanes are decelerated to about 150 mph, and using engine thrust, the aircraft is practically stood on its tail. Would a pilot in combat ever do such a stunt? No, but the point is to show the controllability of the aircraft in slower-speed regimes, which can often get a pilot out of trouble.

The Blues reinvented the high-alpha pass in 1992 when they added a second man to the act, and it became the section high alpha. Some Blue Angel wags have said the high alpha became the section high alpha because up until that point only the opposing solo did the maneuver. When Lt. John Foley moved up to the lead-solo position from the opposing solo, he liked doing it so much that they decided to perform it in section.

Another new maneuver debuting in 1992 was the negative-g push-out on the inverted pass, where the solo pilots do the inverted rolls and then push out of the inverted rolls in negative g.

## Just a Little Respect

Clearly, some of the maneuvers in the show gain more respect among the pilots than others, but it all depends on who you talk to. If it's one of the Diamond pilots, they'll tell you the toughest maneuvers are the Line-Abreast Loop and the Echelon Roll. Foley, one of the solo pilots, reluctantly admitted that the Left Echelon Roll is one of the hardest tricks in the business:

> Any roll into a person is a lot harder because it's negative g—pushing away. Like the Delta Roll, No. 5 happens to be on the left outpost; that's one of the hardest spots to be—No. 3 and No. 4—because they're pushing into you; they're rolling into you, and the further down that chair, the more moment arm you have, and you're really pushing negative. When they used to do it in a four-airplane echelon, that was a very demanding pilot maneuver to do.

The line-abreast maneuver is perhaps not as tough physically, but because it involves five of the pilots lined up horizontally next to one another, the slightest wobble, the tiniest mistake, and the crowd can tell it instantly.

From the soloists standpoint, one of the maneuvers that gets their attention is the Tuckover Roll where the two solos come in simultaneously and roll inverted. Foley describes it from here: "Now you have to fly inverted, form on this guy, and then you do a 270-degree roll—blind. It's very demanding from a pilot's standpoint. It looks OK, too." He also mentioned the Tuckwaway Cross: "It's where we come straight

Blue Angel F/A-18 solo head-on, low pass. *McDonnell Douglas*

at you, we roll away from each other 270 degrees, hold, and do a cross."

## The Hornet and the MiG

Two of the most interesting episodes for the team since the arrival of the Hornet have had to do with the Soviet Union. In 1990, under the command of Blue Angel flight leader Capt. Pat Moneymaker, a jet ride swap was proposed by Valerie Minitsky, bureau chief of the Mikoyan Design Bureau, while at the Kalamazoo airshow.

Minitsky proposed taking Capt. Moneymaker for a ride in the back seat of one of their MiG-29 Fulcrums in exchange for a ride for Minitsky in the back seat of the Blue Angels' two-seater F/A-18, normally used for media rides. This happened before the collapse of communism and the warming of relations. Even so, Moneymaker received approval from his boss, Adm. Richard Dunleavy, for the exchange. Lt. John Foley was selected to fly Minitsky.

All went well until afterward when the State Department and the White House heard about it, and there was considerable political fallout over what had started as an informal pilot-to-pilot conversation. Just a few short years afterward, not only would there have not been a fuss, but the Blue Angels would probably have received commendations, as events are about to tell.

## Flying the Stars and Stripes Over the Kremlin

In less than two years, the greatest irony of all was to occur; in the summer of 1992, the Blue Angels flew over the Kremlin in a State Department-sanctioned tour of former Iron Curtain countries. This was the year that saw the Blue Angels making their first European deployment in nearly two decades. It included their first-ever performance in former Iron Curtain countries, including what was once the Soviet Union. The trip, the Blue Angels say, was filled with surprises—of which obtaining approval for the trip may have been the biggest surprise of all.

The September 1992 tour was a far different experience from the team's last overseas visit in 1973. Back then, the United States was still reeling from the effects of Vietnam, the Cold War was at its paranoiac height, and the Blues were flying the F-4J Phantom II. No one then would have believed that the Navy would send its most coveted squadron to pay a courtesy call on Eastern Europe just 19 years later!

The team's commanding officer and flight leader at the time was Capt. Greg "Rug Dance" Wooldridge in what, at the time, appeared to be his last months in the position. Wooldridge said it took two years to put the history-making four-week tour together and to receive an official seal of approval, but it was all worth it. More than a million people got their first glimpse of the precision flying team in action in Bulgaria and Russia, as well as in Sweden, Finland, England, Italy, and Spain.

## Representing the United — StatesAmbassadors in Blue and Gold

It wasn't just the flying they came to see. "People in Bulgaria and Russia are starving to see anything from America," said Wooldridge. The amount of time people wanted from the team surprised him the most. "This general or that mayor wanted to meet us," he said. "The only time off we had was two or three evenings out of four weeks."

Wooldridge thinks the team's tour impressed people both on the ground and in the air. This is no wonder, as they are considered the US Navy's best recruiting tool and goodwill ambassadors to the world. It was, ironically, this same reputation that caused some problems in getting approval for the trip. Some of the Navy brass wanted to keep the team at home for recruiting purposes. Wooldridge said it wasn't until the military exchange program with Russia became a focal point that the Pentagon and the State Department gave their blessing for the trip.

Some good, old-fashioned capitalist initiative and a possibility for improving the trade deficit also had something to do with getting the tour off the ground. "The trip was used to show off the F/A-18 Hornet to potential foreign buyers," Wooldridge explained. "Mac Air [McDonnell Douglas Aircraft, the Hornet's prime contractor] was excited about getting their product in front of those [people] that buy airplanes for Spain and Italy."

It also didn't hurt to show the countries that had recently purchased Hornets, such as Finland, the bang they got for their many bucks. To this end, the Blues gave the Finnish minister of defense at the time (a woman), a much-coveted ride in the team's two-seater F/A-18.

## Major Numbers

The Blue Angels flew eight F/A-18 Hornets (one more than their usual contingent of seven) that were refueled nearly a dozen times in flight on their overseas expedition. Along with the sleek jets, came two C-130 Hercules transport aircraft filled to their ailerons with extra gear and equipment and a C-9, which carried the 60-member crew, nearly twice that required for domestic operations. Much of the necessary gear and equipment had already been pre-positioned in Europe at Ramstein Air Base in Germany by the Navy. This made it possible for the team to retrieve replacement parts much quicker than if they had needed to be sent over from Stateside.

The Blues also had a little help from their Air Force counterparts, the Thunderbirds, who had been to Europe on deployment in 1991. The

A Blue Angel formation salutes the carrier USS *Lexington* (AVT-16), in a hooks-down, wheels-down, "dirty" configuration. *McDonnell Douglas*

The team passes over scenic Coronado Island, San Diego, California, prior to a performance, May 1987. *McDonnell Douglas*

Thunderbirds gave the Blue Angels a lot of "good gouge," according to Lt. Larry Packer, Blue Angel No. 2 at the time. Wooldridge also noted that the review of the Thunderbirds' trip "helped the team a lot."

Although they flew at a couple of military bases, Wooldridge said the team primarily performed at joint-use civilian and military air fields, such as in Bulgaria and Bucharest, Romania, and the US-Italian base at the naval air station in Siganela, Italy, where they also flew with the equally famed Italian military demonstration team, the Freece Tricolorie.

Packer, right wing, was joined in Sweden by his wife and parents—a highlight of the trip for him. "All trips by family members," Packer quickly pointed out, "were paid for by the individual team members" and not the US Navy or taxpayer.

Packer notes that the people in what were once countries locked behind the cultural wall seemed to be very progressive. He admits to being surprised at how much interest they displayed in the American lifestyle and how much they seemed to be interested in also attaining that quality of life. Packer said:

> I had no idea how they lived their lives. They wanted to be more like us. They wanted us to know that they were no longer under communist rule. [The former Iron Curtain countries]

were very well organized and put on some of the best airshows I'd ever seen. The airshow coordinator wasn't a lieutenant or lieutenant commander. They appointed an air-force general to do the job! They made it happen. They didn't deviate from the Blues' needs. It was very impressive. Airshows in Europe are a big deal.

## What's Next—Bodyguards?

Indeed, they were needed when the Blue Angels were in town. The crowds in Bulgaria were so big and so enthusiastic that 10,000 fans surrounded each of the Blue Angels after the show, treating them like rock stars, rather than American fighter pilots. The mobs were so intense that it was impossible for them to continue signing autographs along the crowd line.

## Don't Interrupt Siesta

Spain, on the other hand, was another matter. Unfortunately for the Blues, the team was scheduled for a mid-day performance—right in the middle of siesta time. Packer said there were only a few thousand Spaniards there to watch. Even the Blue Angels can't always fight tradition.

Weather-wise, the team was lucky during their 1992 European deployment. Departing Europe prior to the downpours and floods that deluged Europe in October, the team had relatively good flying conditions, except in Romania. "The visibility in Bucharest was real-

In the dirty configuration, the team demonstrates close, precision flying. Note the proximity of the wings to the nose of the slot pilot. *McDonnell Douglas*

Solos fly the Mirror Pass. Blue Angel No. 5 flies inverted on the wing of Blue Angel No. 6, giving a mirror-image effect. *McDonnell Douglas*

ly difficult," Wooldridge said. "There was an inversion layer, and they burn soft coal for fuel." These two elements made for poor visibility for flying.

The team missed a few things while they were in Europe. Accustomed to working out everyday with weightlifting equipment to withstand the rigors of pulling sustained g's, the team found that Nautilus equipment in Europe was a little hard to come by. Upper-body strength is essential for a demonstration pilot, especially as they rig the F/A-18's stick pressure at 25 pounds, to help them keep the plane as steady as possible and the movements needed to adjust the aircraft as small as possible during those close-in formations.

LCdr. John Foley said that it's more important to be in good overall condition but physically strong:

> You read tons of articles about g-tolerance. They say high blood pressure helps and all that, but, in reality, like everything, there's a norm. You wouldn't want to be a long-distance, cross-country runner because now your heart is pumping too slow but, on the other hand, you don't want to be lethargic, either. We find the best

thing is weights—free-weight training, and if you're physically strong and in shape, then you can fight the g's off.

## They Wanted Their MTV

Team members say they also missed the freedom of driving themselves and going whenever and wherever they wanted. Television and its constant flow of information was cited by Wooldridge as one of the things he missed the most from the United States.

With the team on the road nearly 300 days a year, one would expect a few squabbles among the team, but Packer said that during the trip, "We all seemed to roll with the punches."

## What Did the Trip Actually Accomplish?

Larry Packer had looked forward to showing the world what US Navy pilots do. "We've got the best training, personnel, and planes, and we're looking forward to showing them," he said. But perhaps John Foley (Blue Angel No. 5, lead solo) summed it up best: "When they look up and see the Blue Angels, what I want them to see is the excellence that we represent is what America represents."

Since 1946, the Blue Angels have demonstrated to more than 250 million people the literal meaning of the word excitement. They have inspired and amazed a countless number of kids, who leave the airshow performing imaginary dogfights with plastic airplane models or just their hands, dreaming that one day they will wear the blue-and-gold patch of the Blue Angels.

They have left normally sane, staid adults jumping up and down from adrenaline after a "sneak pass" or one of the dynamic crossing maneuvers. Despite hands shaking from fatigue after a grueling flight, team members sign autographs and take the time to chat with people of all ages, races, abilities, and attitudes, making their own stories and leaving their own legacies.

Here's looking forward to another 50 years of excellence.

Blue Angels' opposing solo (#6) blasts by in the team's current
aircraft, the F/A-18 Hornet. *US Navy*

# Chapter Nine

# Behind the Scenes with the Blue Angels

You think you are a pretty hot stick. You've accumulated thousands of flight hours in an "airborne weapons systems platform" and made hundreds of No. 3-wire carrier landings. As the commercial said, you've "Been there. Done that." But becoming a member of one of the world's best military flight demonstration teams involves a lot more than just having the right numbers.

Blue Angels crew. These are some of the many people behind the scenes who keep the Blue Angels in the air, on schedule, and looking good. In the background is the team's current transport aircraft, a C-130 Hercules. *US Navy*

## Since When Do Recruiters Fly Jets?

Most people are surprised to discover that the Blue Angels' mission is not just entertaining the public, which they do, but attracting the cream of America's young men and women into service with the US Navy and Marine Corps. Who wouldn't be impressed with the skill that allows a pilot to part your hair with a state-of-the-art fighter with full afterburning jets roaring down the show line?

But why does the Navy need to recruit when, as with all of the military services, it is reducing its numbers since the demise of the Cold War? How often has it been said in the media that the US military of the 1990s is among the smartest, best-trained, best-qualified militaries in history?

The answer to both questions is that the Navy still needs the best and the brightest that the nation has to offer for both its officer and enlisted ranks. Recruiting this top echelon into military service has gotten tougher with reduced opportunities for advancement and no more guarantees of a lifetime career with a good pension awaiting them at the end of a career.

## More Than Fancy Flying

To fulfill their mission, the Blue Angels must, by the very nature of their job, select for certain personality characteristics, as well as the highest flying standards. Demonstration-pilot applicants must have

# Welcome Aboard Fat Albert Airlines

The transport aircraft for the Blue Angels, "Fat Albert Airlines," is a C-130 Hercules, the only Marine Corps aircraft permanently assigned to a Navy squadron for support. It is flown by three Marine Corps pilots with a flight crew of five more Marines. They are the heavy haulers, moving the team's 30-person crew, and any and all parts that an F/A-18 Hornet might need, to and from airshow sites.

The aircraft carries 25,000 pounds of equipment and 45,000 pounds of fuel. It can also be a part of the show when the aircraft performs the spectacular jet-assisted takeoff (JATO, in military slang), during which eight solid-fuel rockets that are strapped to its sides help propel the C-130 off the ground in less than 1,500 feet (half of its normal runway requirement). Climbing at a 45-degree angle until it reaches 1,000 feet, it takes less time to reach that altitude than it took to read this passage.

In September 1991, the Blue Angels received a Navy C-130 that replaced the older C-130 used up to that point. The new aircraft brought about a change to an old paint scheme—the return of the traditional blue and gold. The Blue Angels' name and logo is prominently featured on the aircraft, and you can often see the Stars and Strips flying on top of the C-130.

Air-to-air with Fat Albert. The C-130 is capable of taking everything the team needs while on the road except a spare engine. Groups of approximately 35 crew members travel abroad Fat Albert Airlines from show to show in rotating cycles. Traditionally flown by a Marine-Corps crew, the aircraft often takes part in the air show, performing a JATO (Jet-Assisted Take Off). *US Navy*

at least 1,500 hours in a tactical jet, such as the A-6 Intruder, F-14 Tomcat, F/A-18 Hornet, or the sub-hunter S-3 Viking. They must have flown off of a carrier. For most demo pilots, the

Commander Greg Wooldridge is one of the few to have served twice with the team, both times as commanding officer. *US Navy*

chance for a tour with the Blue Angels usually comes after a few cruises—enough time for a pilot to understand the unique demands placed on a fleet pilot. Pilots are usually in their early- to mid-thirties when they apply to the team.

LCdr. John Foley joined the team as narrator in 1989 and then moved up to opposing solo and then lead solo. He said that it takes about 10 years for a Navy pilot to accumulate enough experience to apply for duty with the Blue Angels. "Most guys have more than that," he noted.

The position of flight leader, more often known as "Boss," is even more rigorous. The requirements demand 3,000 hours, and the applicant must have had command of a tactical squadron. But just being the best fighter jock to ever strap on a g-suit but who can't—or isn't willing to—relate to the public, just won't cut the Blue Angel mustard.

"Obviously, flying is very important to us," said Lt. Larry Packer (No. 2, right wing position), "so is the record of the individual, but personality is a lot of it, too."

Selecting members who already possess polished social skills enables them to withstand the often heavy strain of living in the public eye nearly 100 percent of the time. The coveted Blue Angels patch brings with it a heavy responsibility to live up to the team's standards. These same "people" skills that help them talk to the public without getting tongue-tied also permit them to get along with teammates who are on the road together for up to 290 days a year. Few Blue Angels would argue that they often see their teammates more than their families. The team must become, in a sense, its own family.

Asked to describe the Blue Angels in a single word, two-time Blue Angels leader Greg Wooldridge started to say, "professional," but then he paused because he says it didn't reflect anything special about the team.

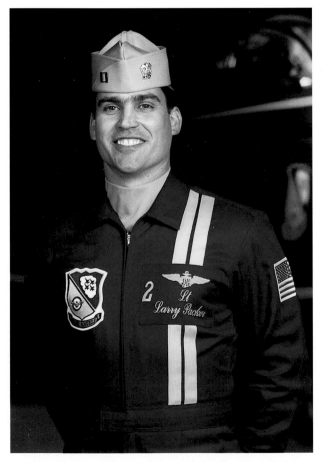

Lieutenant Larry Packer, who flew in the #2 position (right wing) with the Blue Angels. *US Navy*

Lieutenant Commander John Foley flew with the team in both the #6 opposing solo and #5 lead solo positions. *US Navy*

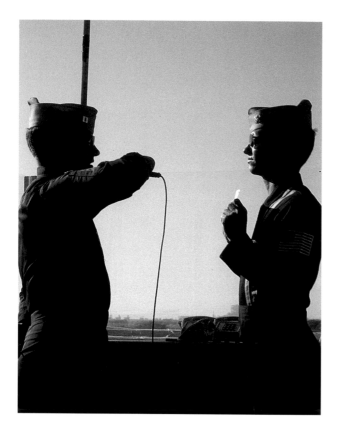

"Personable," is the word he finally chose. Actually, both words are apt. Clearly, these people take their jobs seriously, but there is no "cookie-cutter" personality type on the team.

### Lower, Faster, Closer

The Blue Angel demonstration team of today consists of eight members. Nos. 1 through 6 fly the F/A-18s in the show. No. 7 is the team narrator (who will move up to a show slot the following year), and No. 8 is the events coordinator and is normally a Naval flight officer, (usually a

One of the team's trademarks is its canopy-to-canopy diamond formation, shown here in the Diamond pass. Positions 1-4 fly in the diamond formations. *US Navy*

Blue Angels, Diamond Pass, smoke on. How many hundreds of thousands of rolls of film are shot of the Blue Angels each year. *Armand Veronico*

radar intercept officer from an F-14 Tomcat, or a weapons systems officer from an A-6).

The team is led by No. 1, the Boss, who heads the Blue Angel Diamond formation made up of the first four aircraft; No. 2 is on the right wing, and No. 3 is on the left. No. 4 is the slot position, one of the most difficult positions on the team to fly. Pilot No. 5 is the lead solo, and No. 6 is the opposing solo. When all six fly together, they form the trademark Blue Angel triangle known as the Delta formation.

During a typical 40-minute high show, the team roars through about 29 maneuvers with 15 seconds between each—they don't want the audience to get bored. The maneuvers, the team emphasizes, are the same ones taught to all Navy

pilots—high-speed passes, rolls, loops, join-ups, formation changes, and low-speed applications. These guys just do them lower, faster, and closer together. The Blue Angels take the basics, bring them to new levels of finesse, and bundle them up in a fast-paced show adding a little bit of glitz and good old show-biz glamour.

Take, for instance, the Delta Roll, a maneuver in which the whole triangle of six aircraft do a slow roll while remaining in position. It would be a rare thing to find a squadron of fleet F/A-18s out on a mission engaging in a Delta Roll—it would be a senseless waste of valuable fuel and time and would probably be the last maneuver the squadron's commanding officer ever did. But the roll itself is a basic flight maneuver that is used in combination with various other tactics to both pursue and evade enemy aircraft. The Blue Angels do show the public the ABCs of a Navy pilot's aviation education, but they do it in a way that makes that training look like the most fun, most exhilarating way to earn a living that exists on earth.

The Blue Angels fly as close as a yardstick away, canopy to canopy, at altitudes of a couple of hundred feet and speeds upwards of 400 knots. They do this day in, day out. For instance, during the 1992 show season (which runs from the end of March until the end of November), they flew 60 shows at more than 30 different cities in the United States, plus a month-long deployment to Europe with shows at an additional 16 cities. All of this only happens after the team has put in twice-a-day practices during their three months of winter training in El Centro, where they will fly more than 120 practice shows before they feel they're ready for the public. Also, before every flight (practice or show), the team goes through a 90-minute briefing and an equally long debriefing after the show.

When they are not flying, or watching themselves fly on videotape, they are meeting people, giving kids tours of the famous blue jets, conducting media interviews, or working out in a gym so they can better withstand the heavyweight g-forces that accompany flight in a high-speed combat jet. Although during most maneuvers they may not pull more than +6.5–7 g's, they may do so many times during a show. The average person, without training for g-tolerance, can lose consciousness or "gray out" at around +4 g's. This doesn't even count the stomach-churning negative-g's (when the blood rushes toward your head and you feel weightless). The Blue Angels must often sustain the g-load for a fairly long period of time. Physiologists have compared an hour of this type of flying to the equivalent of a 12-hour day at hard labor.

Are you beginning to get the idea that this is harder than it looks?

"The thing most people don't realize about the Blues," Wooldridge said, "is how much work goes into making what they do look easy. Also, people don't realize how perishable flying skills are. [The Blue Angels]

Lieutenant Larry Packer, Blue Angel #2, and crew at attention during the 1992 NAS Miramar air show. The Blues make a real effort to make sure that the show on the ground is as exciting as the one in the air. The whole effect makes it a completely polished performance. *Marga Fritze*

practice six days a week, practically every day. It's a very unforgiving environment."

## Becoming a Blue

There are approximately 100 people that make up the Blue Angels squadron. Of these, about 85 are enlisted personnel and 16 are officers, of which eight are the demonstration pilots. To become one of those eight, the Naval aviator completes an application around February of any given year. The potential Blue Angel candidate must obtain a recommendation from as high a command level as possible.

"You need your commanding officer's recommendation; you need a recommendation from people who can support you," Foley said. "It can be an admiral, it can be a CAG [air wing commander—formerly known as air group commander but the old acronym stuck]—someone who says, 'Hey, I think he'll not only be a good pilot but a good representative of our country. We want him to go out there and be a Blue Angel.'"

All of the paperwork then goes to the team, who select the best of these and invite them to become "applicants." Once a candidate becomes an applicant, they begin a process known as "rushing," which is somewhat similar to joining a fraternity—a close approximation to what becoming a Blue Angel is all about.

The rushing process involves meeting each of the current team members on a social as well as professional basis. Applicants are invited to attend nearby airshows and sit in on briefings. "[Applicants] will come in and they get to sit in on briefs, get to see how we operate, go to the functions afterwards, meet the kids, get to see that there's more to this job than just flying," said Foley.

Also like a fraternity, the Blue Angels pick their own members. With the exception of the team leader, there is no one back at HQ looking over their shoulders, telling them whom to select.

The process extends over several months, giving applicants a good chance to watch the team at several airshows. It also gives them the opportunity to see whether or not the applicant will like the other team members. At the same time, the team members are watching the applicant to find out how well he handles himself in public.

By June, the Blue Angels end the applicant involvement at airshows and sit down to make the hard decisions that must be made. Out of all the applicants, perhaps only two or three can be selected for the team.

After selecting eight to ten finalists, the team invites them to Pensacola in July for a week of additional interviews, both formal and informal. After that, Foley said, comes the hard part: "The bottom line is we pick our own guys. Eight of us sit around a table [and] we vote on who's going to replace us."

## The Winners Are . . .

The new team members are announced in October. They are then sent to Jacksonville to be

One of the most difficult maneuvers to make look perfect for the audience is the Line Abreast Loop. If one of the five is even slightly out of position, it will show on the ground. Also, the maneuver has an optical illusion—what the pilots see up in the air is different than what the audience is seeing. The team must adjust the maneuver accordingly. *US Navy*

initiated into the mysteries of the F/A-18 Hornet. They are sent to the RAG (Replacement Air Group), where they learn the basic requirements of how to fly the airplane. After that, they report for duty at NAS Pensacola for additional training. "The one thing about a pilot at this level is, once you're flying in a tactical jet and you have so many thousands of hours, it's not that hard to transition from airplane to airplane," Foley explained. "Airplanes are basically the same."

Blue Angel demonstration pilots still serve two-year stints. But they do not all change over at once. New members are rotated in so there is never an entirely "new" team. The exception to the two-year duty is the narrator. After one year as narrator (No. 7), the pilot usually moves up to

Solos opposing knife-edge pass. The solo pilots push the high-performance envelope of the F/A-18 Hornet. *US Navy*

It doesn't get much closer—the two canopies of the #5 and #6 jets (opposing and lead solo, respectively) are mere inches away. *US Navy*

one of the Nos. 2 through 6 positions for an additional two years. But most years see two or three new demonstration pilots added to the team.

Even though the No. 7 pilot is fully qualified, he is not considered a "spare." If one of the six Blue Angel pilots gets sick, the show goes on with five performers instead. The one guy they can't fly without is the Boss since so many maneuvers are flown off of the Boss's wing—while the Boss looks out ahead, the rest of the team is looking only at the aircraft next to them. Said Foley:

> What happens is, we have no spare guy, and the reason is because the precision is such that unless you do it everyday and you train for it every single day, then you just can't jump in and do it at that level, so it's a proficiency thing, and even within the demo [pilots] there's one, two solos—5 and 6. If one of us gets sick, we've got a single solo—nobody can jump in there. If one of the Diamond guys gets sick, we just leave a hole wherever he is. The only guy that kills us is the boss.

Occasionally, a Blue Angel is called upon to return to service, such as was the case with Wooldridge when he returned the year immediately following the end of his official tour in 1992. The reason for the unusual move was that Capt. Bob Stumpf, Wooldridge's successor as team leader, had been temporarily assigned to administrative duties during the scandal that rocked the Navy, the infamous Tailhook Convention. Stumpf's standing was eventually restored, and he went on to command the team. Another recent unusual move was the team's request that slot pilot LCdr. Scott Anderson stay on for a third year.

An even more unusual step was taken in 1995 when, at the beginning of the season, the Blue Angels canceled their first public appearance of the year at the Phoenix 500 Air Races at Williams Air Force Base outside of Phoenix, Arizona. Team leader Cdr. Donnie Cochran, another one of the few Blue Angels to serve more than once on the team, felt that the team hadn't had enough practice to fly the first show of the season at an unfamiliar show site.

Few pilots make the team after their first year of rushing; most take two years to make the team. For some pilots, it's a matter of

MCAS El Toro, 1994: A crew member is responsible for making sure Lt. Rick Young's jet is ready to roll. Each jet's crew and crew chief are held accountable for their work in a very unique way. The pilots leave the preflight inspection of the aircraft to them, demonstrating the high levels of trust the pilots have in the skill of the crew. *Marga Fritze*

racking up the necessary number of minimum flight hours. For others, the field of applicants might be more competitive one year than the next.

Interestingly enough, talk to the team members and almost all of them express surprise that they were selected. Simple modesty or honest reaction? Probably a combination. One thing is certain—none of the selected applicants know whether or not they've been picked until the team chooses to tell them. The team members responsible for making the selections are famous for their poker faces and strive to give no hint of anyone's status. The first an applicant knows he has been selected is when he receives the "phone call."

For John Foley, becoming a member of the Blue Angels was a goal for him, but his love of aviation started much earlier:

> I just remember my dad took me to an airshow, and I was so young [that] I didn't know what it was, but I looked up there and I went, "This is neat!" It was just something, as a kid, that was in my heart. As I grew, I got smarter

The glamorous part of the job. Being a Blue Angel is as much about savvy public relations skills as flying, Lieutenant Larry Packer signs autographs for several fans following another grueling performance at the 1992 NAS Miramar air show. Physiologists have compared the amount of physical strain the pilots go through during a 45-minute performance to working an eight-hour day at hard labor. After meeting the public, the pilots go into a debrief session on their flight that can last another two hours. *Marga Fritze*

and realized that this was something I might want to do. I just wanted to fly airplanes. Initially I thought about the Air Force because that's what you think about when you think about airplanes. Then, as I got into high school, I got smarter. I saw movies; I saw the airplanes landing on carriers, and I thought, *Man, if you're going to fly, I want to land on carriers.* That looks fun—that looks dandy! Then I went into the Navy and learned to fly jets off a carrier, and once I did that, I said, "This is great." Of course, the Blue Angels was always a goal, but you never think you're ever going to get there—it's just something that's out there, and you just work hard day by day and, all of a sudden, I said, "You know, I'd like to do that," and it just worked out.

## Picking the Boss

Selecting the squadron leader for the Blue Angels follows a slightly different path. But one factor remains the same: Most of the pilots rushing the Blues believe that other

Lead solo, #5, takes off during the 1993 NAS Miramar air show. Some of the show openers, such as the Dirty Roll on takeoff, are as difficult as anything you'll see in the rest of the show and gain a lot respect from other pilots. *Marga Fritze*

The first maneuver of the current show is the Diamond formation rolling out for takeoff. After pulling the wheels off the ground, the Blue Angels boss, #1, will call for a loop. The "Burner Loop", as it's called, takes a lot of skill to maintain the inches of separation between each of the four aircraft. *Marga Fritze*

applicants are more qualified, as was the case with Capt. Wooldridge.

After seeing the first "solicitation" (the application announcement), which comes out in March, he thought, *Gee, that would be neat and fun, but I would never have a chance.* However, a nudging from his junior officers, plus a nagging "what if" plaguing him in the back of his mind, encouraged him to apply. "You never know what would have happened if you don't apply," he kept telling himself.

The requirements for a Blue Angel commanding officer are that you must be in command of a tactical squadron (a prerequisite instituted around 1977, Wooldridge says) and you must be available for a new assignment. The leader must have a minimum of 3,000 flight

hours. There is no minimum number of carrier landings, but with that many hours, they figure the applicant must have a pretty good number of "traps."

Selected for interviews with the other 10–15 Boss applicants, Wooldridge went to Corpus Christi, former home of the Blues, for an interview. After meeting the competition, Wooldridge said he thought the others were more qualified. His mistaken conclusion turned out to be a blessing in disguise.

"I thought, *There is no way I'm going to be selected,* so I was really relaxed. I was going to enjoy myself," he recalls. He was entirely at ease during the meetings, both professional and social, in a very pressure-packed situation. This, plus the deep concern he felt for the people who work for

One of the most aesthetic parts of the Blue Angels show is the Echelon Pass, with the Diamond (#1-4) tightly stacked. Note that the smoke is being emitted on the left side of the aircraft only. *Marga Fritze*

him, he believes impressed the selectors, including the chief of Naval Air Training.

What kind of a person would Wooldridge choose to replace himself? "Down-to-earth, but not too rough around the edges," he laughed. "Compassion and caring and concern are very important," he added. Following his tour with the Blues, which ended in December 1992, Wooldridge was scheduled to take up command

of the US Naval Air Station at Rota, Spain, a plum assignment. Unfortunately, politics intervened and he returned to lead the Blues for a third year until his replacement, Bob Stumpf, was cleared to take over the team.

What does a Blue Angel Boss do after his glory days with the Blues are finished? There are three courses available to the officer (usually a captain in rank): command of a naval air station, command of a carrier air wing (consisting of several squadrons) or command of a deep-draft (a large Navy support ship), after which you become qualified to take command of a carrier.

### Practice Makes Perfect

After a pilot has been named to the team and has been released from his squadron, the new demonstration team member reports to Pensacola for the really serious training. Beginning with solo flights, which progress into two-aircraft flights, new pilots (called "nubies") begin flying demonstration maneu-

NAWS Pt. Mugu, 1993. Former Blue Angel and now Adm. Bill Newman (left) was in charge of Pt. Mugu at the time this photograph was taken, and has since been transferred to Pentagon duty. Admiral, Newman is surrounded by his wife and Admiral's aide. The Blue Angels take special pride in "Once a Blue Angel, Always a Blue Angel." This particular show is unique in that there were two military demonstration teams flying: the Blues and the Canadian Snowbirds. *Marga Fritze*

Shown at their winter training base at El Centro, California, the team taxis in for recovery after performing for the local media at the beginning of the season. *Marga Fritze*

vers at high altitudes, gradually flying them lower and faster.

Just as the Three Sea Hawks learned back in the early days of formation flying, by beginning their training in the relative safety of higher altitudes, pilots adjust to the demanding precision and split-second timing. One of the hardest adjustments to the demands of demonstration team flying, pilots report, is acquiring the intense level of physical and mental concentration required for the job.

## Eeney, Meeney, Miney, Mo

In the meantime, the team and the Pentagon's Powers-That-Be have received sacks full of performance requests from airshows nationwide. Blue Angels No. 7 and No. 8 hit the road to check out potential show sites. Each air field must meet stringent requirements to ensure the team's safety.

For example, there must be emergency equipment on site, and there must be an arresting-gear system (similar to that used on board aircraft carriers to help stop a jet in a matter of yards) within 50 miles of the site in case one of the aircraft suffers a problem that requires assistance with landing. Sometimes, the arresting gear is used merely as a precaution, such as at the show the Blues put on for the media at their win-

ter training site in El Centro in 1991, when part of the hydraulic system on the No. 1 aircraft (Wooldridge's) failed. Although the F/A-18 is fully "redundant" (meaning it has several backups), Wooldridge trapped his jet using the arresting gear located on the NAS El Centro runways. In a matter of a few minutes, the crew had him out of his jet and into the spare jet, kept ready for just such a situation. It happened so quickly and was handled so efficiently that most of the media present remained oblivious to the event.

After the field inspections, the Pentagon then selects the fortunate civilian and military airshows the Blues will fly, making sure that there are no conflicts with the team's Air Force counterparts, the Thunderbirds. In fact, there is a rule which states that the show sites where the teams fly must be at least 100 miles apart. The eagerly awaited schedule is usually released in November, in time for the International Council of Air Shows convention.

## Hit the Road, Jack

The first Monday in January is moving day for the Blues. Having already sent a lot of gear and crew members aboard the team's C-130 Hercules transport—"Fat Albert Airlines"—to their winter training grounds at NAS El Centro, the F/A-18s depart for their temporary desert home.

# The Organizational Structure of the Blue Angels

The squadron consists of several departments or "work centers" for the approximately 85 enlisted personnel:

Maintenance: Responsible for the upkeep of the Blue Angel aircraft. This department is further divided into specialized shops working on systems such as engine repair or electronics.

Supply: These people make sure that all the aircraft parts and supplies needed by seven very complicated jets are ready and available.

Public Affairs: They make sure you know when and where the team will be performing. They are responsible for all of the squadron's marketing and public-information efforts. Any time a member of the media wants to find out about the team or talk to one of its members, these are the people who make it happen.

Events Coordinators Office: The assistant events coordinators are like the Blue Angels' own travel agency. They make sure that all hotels for the crew and hangars and ground support for the aircraft are arranged at each airshow location.

Medical: The hospital corpsman works with the flight surgeon in making sure the medical needs of all the squadron personnel are taken care of.

C-130: The transport aircraft, "Fat Albert Airlines," is a C-130 Hercules, the only Marine Corps aircraft permanently assigned to a Navy squadron for support. It is flown by three Marine Corps pilots with a flight crew of five more Marines.

---

Located about two hours driving time east of San Diego, El Centro provides plenty of sunny, reliable weather and miles of room in which to fly without worrying about breaking any windows. There is also, as anyone who has been there can testify, little in the El Centro area to distract pilots from their flying.

## Every Step You Take . . .

To the public, the Blue Angels are the six pilots flying in synchronous syncopation in their high-tech steeds. Few ever realize how many other people are needed to keep the stable of aircraft flying.

Besides the eight demonstration pilots, there are three US Marine Corps C-130 transport pilots and five other officers charged with making sure everything runs smoothly. Specialists in maintenance, logistics, supplies, and public relations, and a flight surgeon are all major components of the team. Each year, about three jet pilots, three staff officers, and a C-130 pilot from the Marine Corps are rotated into the squadron. Blue Angels Nos. 1–6, No. 8, the maintenance officer, and the flight surgeon serve for two years; the other officers serve for three.

The various officers are also responsible for the nearly 100 enlisted personnel assigned to the team. The maintenance officer, for example, oversees the crew chiefs assigned to each aircraft and the specialists who provide the team with expert skills in such areas as engine repair, electrical systems, and avionics.

Each and every one of these people—men and women—are considered Blue Angels, not just the pilots who get most of the public's attention.

Not all members of the squadron are on the road all the time. Approximately 30 enlisted personnel travel aboard "Fat Albert" in rotating groups. Each group is on the road for around two weeks at a time.

## You've Got to Believe

One of the Blue Angels' traditions emphasizes just how important each crew member is. Normally, a Navy pilot will perform a "walk-down" and flight-control check of their aircraft prior to takeoff, like a cowboy checks his saddle girth. Pilots have a need to know that no mysterious objects have found their way into engine air inlets and that nothing has jammed a control surface.

The Blues, however, assign the pre-flight checks to their ground crews, not out of laziness but because the practice involves the ground crew in the responsibility for the safety of both pilot and aircraft. They do it because it reflects the ground crew's exacting standards. Knowing that they've got the best ground crew in the fleet, the pilots trust them implicitly.

Enlisted personnel, usually on board with the team for three years, go through just as exhaustive a selection process as the officers. All are at least a senior E-5 (petty officer 2nd class in the Navy) or sergeant (in the Marine Corps) rank. They also must volunteer for the duty. In addition, they must be career oriented, show consistent superior performance in their previous assignments, and be recommended by their commanding officer. The crew is as big a part of the show as the pilots, and they practice just as hard. Every step they take is timed to make even the most mundane task look exciting, all of which helps in recruiting future maintenance crew talent.

## We're Outta Here

Finally, after the hours of practice and briefings, the show season officially begins at El Centro. The Blues put on a special show for the local people who have put up with nearly three months of eardrum-splitting fly-bys. Then the Blues and their families pack up and head back to Pensacola, where they will be based during the season's round of shows. Shows are flown on the weekends, so on Mondays the team rests. On Tuesdays, the demonstration pilots attend an "all officers meeting." Wednesday is usually another practice day and the day on which the No. 7 and No. 8 pilots depart for the next show site to make sure everything is in readiness for the rest of the team's arrival. On Thursday, the team with the other six jets and "Fat Albert" with approximately 35 crew, spare parts, and everyone's luggage, takes off for the next show site, a cycle repeated during the April to November months. The exception to this is during the team's West Coast appearances, when they try to go to two or three shows in a row, in which case they won't return to Pensacola until after the shows.

## "Mark It"

As the F/A-18s arrive at the show site, they perform what are called "circle and arrival" maneuvers before landing, during which they check the visual reference points they will use during their actual shows. The soloists use stop watches mounted in the cockpits to set their "marks"—points when the opposing aircraft must be spotted in order to safely perform the head-on maneuvers. Later that day, the team might fly a practice

show, conduct media interviews, and be the star attractions at a charity event.

After visiting local schools and hospitals on Friday, the team flies an afternoon demonstration at military base show sites for military members and their dependents, recruiters, the disabled, and the elderly who might have trouble moving about in the crowds the Blues inevitably draw over the weekend. This kind of community involvement is one of the hallmarks of the Blue Angels. Since the team normally performs for two days (rather than the usual one-day performances by the Thunderbirds), they have a little more time to make the visits that mean so much to kids in school or in a hospital. You never know: One of those kids might someday be the one in the blue-and-gold flight suits, inspiring others to stay in school.

Finally, after attending enough cocktail parties to wear down the most ardent partygoers, the Blue Angels are ready to get down to business on Saturday and Sunday. But it's still not a case of "hop in the jet, hit the burners, and then let's go have a beer." After each show, the team takes time to sign autographs for fans on the crowd line. They may also give a special group a tour of the aircraft at that time. It's not over yet—they still have a no-holds-barred debriefing to go through. "People think we're going to get something to eat after we sign autographs at the crowd line," Wooldridge said. Not true—they are on their way to a two-hour critique of their performance. Knowing that their lives are on the line tends to open up the lines of communication. In order to assure that what they hear is the truth and nothing but the truth, the Blue Angel debriefings are sacrosanct; outsiders are barred.

After two grueling days of high-speed maneuvers, the show closes and Blues prepare to pack up and fly home. The aircraft depart either on Sunday night or Monday morning, depending on distances to fly and time schedules.

Either way, on Tuesday morning, it starts all over again.

## After the Blues

There is no such thing as a "former" Blue

Symmetry in motion: the Blue Angels diamond performs the Echelon Pass during the 1994 MCAS El Toro air show. *Marga Fritze*

Angel—once you've made it into this elite club, you are a member for life (there's an association of them). All Blue Angels take special pride in maintaining and perpetuating the myths and traditions that have been such an integral part of the squadron during its 50 years.

In the near-term, however, following their "separation" from the squad, the pilot returns to the fleet. A fairly recent requirement for Blue Angels is that they must serve an additional two years of duty at the end of their assignment to the team. For their next tour, many of the demonstration pilots go either to a fighter/attack squadron at NAS Jacksonville or one at NAS Lemoore.

---

*Blue Angels*

# Becoming A Navy Pilot

Before you can even think about joining the Blue Angels, there is still one basic requirement: You have to be a Naval Aviator. There are several ways to accomplish this, although with shrinking defense budgets and changing world orders, it is getting harder and harder to get one of the fewer and fewer slots.

One way to pursue your dreams of entering into the high-Mach wonderland is to wrangle yourself into the Naval Academy at Annapolis, Maryland. Many fighter pilots—and many Blue Angels—have chosen this route. You can also attend a private college and join the Naval Reserve Officer Training Corps program (NROTC). If you already have a college degree from elsewhere, you can be sent to the 14-week Aviation Officer Candidate School (AOCS), which includes six weeks of Aviation Indoctrination or ground school where you'll study aerodynamics, navigation, flight physiology, and water and land survival. Some 1,400 people go through AOCS a year, but nearly one out of four drop out in the first week. Another way is to join Naval Aviation Cadets (NavCads, who have at least two years of college). NavCads receive their commission only after completing flight training—on the same day they receive their wings. If a NavCad fails aviator training, they still have to finish out their commitment to the military, but as an enlisted member.

Once the basic obligations are fulfilled (no easy matter), it's time for the next phase of your training. Give yourself 18 months and 270 flight hours and you, too, can be a Navy pilot.

Basic or primary flight training takes place at NAS Whiting Field, Florida, or NAS Corpus Christi, Texas, in Beech T-34C Mentors. If you survive this and do well, you can then hope to be selected for a slot learning to fly the exotic birds: fighter or attack aircraft.

If you are one of the lucky few, you go on to become an Advanced selectee, which means you'll fly an F-14 Tomcat, F/A-18 Hornet, A-6 Intruder, EA-6, or an S-3 Viking.

Reporting for basic jet training at one of four training wings either at NAS Pensacola; NAS Meridian, Mississippi; or Kingsville or Beesville, Texas, you'll study meteorology, communications, aerodynamics, engineering, and navigation and put in some time with the simulators. Next comes the fun stuff: formation flying, aerobatics, and instrument flight rules (IFR) flight (although some humorists say it stands for "I Follow Roads," IFR flight means you navigate by means of instruments and radio contact with controllers).

Finally, there is gunnery and the fearsome carrier qualification aboard the training carrier.

Following a course in intermediate-strike training in a T-2C Buckeye, you will head for advanced strike training in the Douglas T45-A Goshawk—a British Aerospace Hawk with a tailhook added.

Lastly, you'll have 108 hours in the AT-4 Skyhawk and 68 hours in simulators. Here, you'll be refining your flying skills and military tactics, learning to accurately aim bombs, rockets, and bullets at a ground target. You'll also experience the thrill of low-level flying (giving you a small taste of what the Blue Angels do all the time), hone up your dogfighting, and put in more time on the carrier.

All of this is followed by assignment to a RAG, or fleet replenishment squadron, and then to be assigned to a front-line squadron.

The 1992 Blue Angel team. *US Navy*

Several Blue Angels have gone on to achieve flag rank in the service (including E.L. Feightner, Bill Newman, and Tony Less). Others sought out their fame and fortune in other industries, such as Duke Vincent, now a television producer. Still more are test pilots with aerospace companies, such as Gary "Bear" Smith, Kevin O'Mara, and Tim Dineen with McDonnell Douglas. And, like so many military pilots, many Blue Angels now strap into the left seat in the cockpit of an airliner, such as Jack Ekl and Vance Parker. Some former Blues still fly in airshows, only this time as civilians. When Ekl isn't eking out a living flying airliners, he pours himself into a tiny BD-5 jet, flying aerobatic routines for a beer-company sponsor. Bill "Burner" Beardsley also flies the microjet—about the size of a shoe box.

One thing is for certain, once you get to be a Blue Angel, it's hard to get airplanes out of your system.

# Appendix I

## Aircraft Specifications and Bureau Numbers

|  | **F6F** | **F8F** |
| --- | --- | --- |
| Length | 33' 7" | 28' 3" |
| Wing Span | 42' 10" | 35' 10" |
| Wing Area (sq. ft.) | 334 | 244 |
| Height | 13' 1" | 13' 10" |
| Max. Takeoff Weight (lb.) | 15,413 | 12,947 |
| Powerplant | R-2800-10W | R-2800-34W |

|  | **F9F-5** | **F9F-8** | **F11F** | **F-4** |
| --- | --- | --- | --- | --- |
| Length | 33' 10" | 41' 9" | 46' 11.25" | 58' 2" |
| Wing Span | 38' 0" | 34' 6" | 31' 7.5" | 38' 5" |
| Wing Area (sq. ft.) | 250 | 337 | 250 | 530 |
| Height | 12' 3" | 12' 3" | 13' 2.75" | 16' 3" |
| Max. Takeoff Weight (lb.) | 18,721 | 19,738 | 22,160 | 56,000 |
| Powerplant | J-48-P-6A | J-48-P-8A | J-65-W-18 | 2 x J-79-GE-10 |
| Static Thrust (lb.) | 6,250 | 7,250 | 7,450 | 11,970ea. |

|  | **A-4F** | **F/A-18** |
| --- | --- | --- |
| Length | 40' 1.5" | 56' 0" |
| Wing Span | 27' 6" | 40' 4.75" |
| Wing Area | 260 | 400 |
| Height | 15' 2" | 15' 3.5" |
| Max. Takeoff Weight (lb.) | 24,500 | 56,000 |
| Powerplant | J-52-P-408 | 2 x F404-GE-400 |
| Static Thrust (lb.) | 11,200 | 16,000ea. |

## Aircraft Specifications
## Bureau Numbers of Team Aircraft
### Grumman F6F-5 Hellcat
79049
79393
79914
80097
### North American SNJ Texan
44008
91047
112193
### Grumman F8F-1 Bearcat
94781
94880
94843
94969
94985
94986
94989
94990
94992
94996
95000
95021
95037
95124
95134
95144
95187

### Grumman F9F-2 Panther
122585
122587
122588
122589
123016
123017
### Chance Vought F7U-1
124426
124427
### Grumman F9F-5 Panther
125239
125249
125258
125278
125283
125286
125294
125305
125327
125943
125989
125993
126070
126071
126101

## Grumman F9F-6, -8B, -8T Cougar

128080
128116
128128
128129
128152
128446
131099
131142
131143
131147
131205
131208
131210
131211
131212
131213
138870
144279
144368
142470
147404

## Grumman F11F Tiger

138633
138639
138640
138641
138642
138643
138644
138645
138647
141738
141764
141765
141775
141777
141790
141797

## Grumman F11F Tiger

141802
141811
141812
141816
141823
141829
141831
141837
141847
141849
141850
141851
141853
141859
141863
141867
141868
141872
141873
141874
141876
141882
141883
141884

## McDonnell Douglas F-4J Phantom II

153072
153075
153076
153077
153078
153079
153080
153081
153082
153083
153084
153085
153086
153839

## McDonnell Douglas A-4F, TA-4J Skyhawk II

154175
154176
154177
154179
154180
154217
154383
154904
154975
154983
154984
154985
154986
154992
155029
155033
155056
155502
153477
158107
158722

## McDonnell Douglas F/A-18

161519
161520
161521
161523
161524
161525
161526
161527
161528
161353
161354
161355
161366
161931
161932
161941

## McDonnell Douglas F/A-18

161943
161945
161952
161955
161957
161962
161973
161975
161978
161983
161984
161985

## Support Aircraft

Curtiss R5C-1: 39507
Douglas R4D-6: 17123, 17281
Douglas R4D-7: 99838
Douglas R4D-8: 12437
Douglas R5D-2: 50868, 56508
Douglas R5D-3: 91996
Douglas R5D-5R: 90407
Lockheed C-121J: 131623
Lockheed TV-2: 128662, 128676, 137955
Lockheed C-130: 149806, 150690, 151891

# Appendix II

## Roster of Officers, 1946–95

**Flight Members**

| Name | Show Seasons |
|---|---|
| *Cdr. R.M. "Butch" Voris | 1946–47/52 |
| Lt. J.W. Barnitz | 1946–47 |
| Lt. (j.g.) Robby Robinson | 1946 |
| Lt. Mel Cassidy | 1946 |
| Lt. (j.g.) Gale Stouse | 1946 |
| Lt. Wick Wickendoll | 1946–47 |
| Lt. Al Taddeo | 1946–47 |
| Lt. Chuck Knight | 1946–47 |
| Lt. Bob Thelen | 1947–48 |
| *LCdr. Bob Clarke | 1946–48 |
| Lt. (j.g.) Billy May | 1946–48 |
| Lt. Hal Heagerty | 1947–49 |
| Lt. Bob Longworth | 1948–49 |
| Lt. Ed Mahood | 1949 |
| Lt. Ed Oliphant | 1949–50 |
| Lt. Ralph Hanks | 1950 |
| Lt. George Hoskins | 1948–50 |
| Lt. (j.g.) Fritz Roth | 1948–50 |
| *LCdr. Dusty Rhodes | 1947–50 |
| *LCdr. Johnny Magda | 1949–50 |
| Lt. Jake Robcke | 1948–50 |
| Lt. Bud Wood | 1952 |
| LCdr. E. L. "Whitey" Feightner | 1952 |
| Lt. "Mac" MacKnight | 1948–49/52–53 |
| Lt. Pat Murphy | 1952–53 |
| Lt. Tom Jones | 1952 |
| Lt. Buddy Rich | 1952–53 |
| Lt. Auz Auzland | 1953–54 |
| Lt. Frank Jones | 1952–53 |
| *LCdr. Ray Hawkins | 1948–50/ 52–53 |
| LCdr. Frank Graham | 1949–50/52–53 |
| Capt. Chuck Hiett, USMC | 1954 |
| Capt. Pete Olson, USMC | 1955 |
| Lt. Red Riedl | 1955 |

**Flight Members**

| Name | Show Seasons |
|---|---|
| Lt. Dayl Crow | 1953–54 |
| LCdr. Dick Newhafer | 1949/54–55 |
| Capt. Chuck Holloway, USMC | 1956 |
| Capt. Ed Rutty, USMC | 1955 |
| Lt. Lefty Schwartz | 1956–57 |
| Lt. Bill Gureck | 1955–56 |
| Lt. Nello Pierozzi | 1955–57 |
| Lt. Bruce Bagwell | 1955–57 |
| *Cdr. Zeke Cormier | 1954–56 |
| Lt. Ed McKellar | 1953–56 |
| *Cdr. Ed Holley | 1957–58 |
| Cdr. Nick Glasgow | 1958 |
| 1st Lt. Tom Jefferson, USMC | 1957 |
| Lt. Mark Perrault | 1957–59 |
| Lt. Skip Campanella | 1959 |
| Lt. Don McKee | 1959 |
| Capt. Stoney Mayock, USMC | 1958–59 |
| Lt. John Damian | 1958–59 |
| LCdr. Jack Dewenter | 1958–59 |
| Lt. Herb Hunter | 1957–59 |
| Lt. Bob Rasmussen | 1957–59 |
| Lt. Bill Sherwood | 1959 |
| Lt. Chuck Elliott | 1960 |
| Lt. John Rademacher | 1960 |
| Lt. Duke Ventigmiglia | 1960–61 |
| Lt. Bill Rennie | 1960–61 |
| *Cdr. Zeb Knott | 1959–61 |
| Capt. Doug McCaughey, USMC | 1960–62 |
| Lt. Hank Giedzinski | 1961–62 |
| Lt. Lew Chatham | 1961–63 |
| Lt. Dan MacIntyre | 1961–63 |
| Lt. George Neale | 1962–64 |
| Lt. Dick Langford | 1962–64 |
| Capt. John Kretsinger, USMC | 1963–64 |
| LCdr. Bob Cowles | 1963–65 |
| Lt. Bob McDonough | 1964–65 |

## Flight Members

| Name | Show Seasons |
|---|---|
| Lt. Mike Van Ort | 1966 |
| LCdr. Dick Oliver | 1964-66 |
| Lt. Frank Mezzadri | 1964-66 |
| *Cdr. Bob Aumack | 1964-66 |
| Lt. Frank Gallagher | 1967 |
| Capt. Ron Thompson, USMC | 1967 |
| Capt. Fred Craig, USMC | 1965-67 |
| Lt. Red Hubbard | 1965-67 |
| Lt. Dave Rongering | 1966-67 |
| Lt. Norm Gandia | 1966-67 |
| Lt. Fred Wilson | 1966-68 |
| Lt. Hal Loney | 1967-68 |
| Lt. Bill Worley | 1968 |
| Lt. Smokey Tolbert | 1968 |
| Capt. Vince Donile, USMC | 1967-69 |
| Lt. John Allen | 1967-69 |
| Lt. Rick Millson | 1968-69 |
| Lt. Rick Adams | 1968-69 |
| *Cdr. Bill Wheat | 1967-69 |
| Lt. Ernie Christensen | 1969-70 |
| Lt. Steve Shoemaker | 1969-70 |
| Lt. Dick Schram | 1969-71 |
| Lt. Jim Maslowski | 1970-71 |
| Capt. Kevin O'Mara, USMC | 1970-71 |
| LCdr. J. D. Davis | 1970-71 |
| *Cdr. Harley Hall | 1970-71 |
| Lt. Lou Lalli | 1970-72 |
| Lt. Larry Watters | 1972 |
| Lt. Gary "Bear" Smith | 1972 |
| Lt. Bill Switzer | 1971-72 |
| Lt. Bill Beardsley | 1971-72 |
| *LCdr. Don Bently | 1972-73 |
| Capt. Mike Murphy, USMC | 1972-73 |
| Lt. Steve Lambert | 1972-73 |
| *LCdr. Skip Umstead | 1970-73 |
| Lt. Chuck Newcomb | 1972-74 |
| Capt. John Fogg, USMC | 1973-74 |

## Flight Members

| Name | Show Seasons |
|---|---|
| LCdr. Marlin Witta | 1973-74 |
| *Capt. Ken Wallace | 1954-55/61-63/74 |
| Lt. John Chehansky | 1973-75 |
| *Cdr. Tony Less | 1974-75 |
| Lt. Denny Sapp | 1975-76 |
| Lt. John Patton | 1974-76 |
| Capt. Bill Holverstott, USMC | 1975-76 |
| Lt. Nile Kraft | 1976 |
| Lt. Jim Bauer | 1975-77 |
| Lt. Al Cisneros | 1975-77 |
| LCdr. Vance Parker | 1974-75/77 |
| *Cdr. K. C. "Casey" Jones | 1976-77 |
| Lt. Ray Sandelli | 1977-78 |
| Lt. Mike Curtin | 1978 |
| LCdr. John Miller | 1976-78 |
| LCdr. Don Simmons | 1977-78 |
| Capt. Dan Keating, USMC | 1977-78 |
| LCdr. Jerry Tucker | 1973-74/79 |
| LCdr. Bruce Davey | 1977-79 |
| *Cdr. Bill Newman | 1978-79 |
| Lt. Kent Horne | 1979-80 |
| LCdr. Mike Nord | 1978-80 |
| Maj. Fred Stankovich, USMC | 1979-80 |
| LCdr. Jack Ekl | 1979-81 |
| LCdr. Jim Horsley | 1980-81 |
| *Cdr. Denny Wisely | 1980-81 |
| Lt. Bud Hunsucker | 1981-82 |
| Lt. Randy Clark | 1980-82 |
| LCdr. Stu Powrie | 1981 |
| LCdr. Bob Stephens | 1981-82 |
| Lt. Kevin Miller | 1981-83 |
| Maj. Tim Dineen, USMC | 1981-82 |
| LCdr. Jim Ross | 1979-80/82-83 |
| *Cdr. Dave Carroll | 1982-83 |
| LCdr. John Virden | 1983-84 |

## Flight Members

| Name | Show Seasons |
|------|-------------|
| LCdr. Chris Ives | 1983–84 |
| LCdr. Scott Anderson | 1982–84 |
| Maj. Mark Lauritzen, USMC | 1983–84 |
| LCdr. Mike Gershon | 1984–85 |
| Lt. Anthony P. Caputi | 1984–85 |
| *Cdr. Larry Pearson | 1984–85 |
| Maj. Bill Campbell, USMC | 1985–86 |
| LCdr. Curt Watson | 1983–86 |
| LCdr. Pat Walsh | 1985–87 |
| Capt. Mark Bircher, USMC | 1985–87 |
| LCdr. David Anderson | 1985–87 |
| Lt. Mike Campbell | 1987–88 |
| LCdr. Wayne Molnar | 1986–88 |
| *Capt. Gil Rud | 1986–88 |
| LCdr. Cliff Skelton | 1987–89 |
| LCdr. Mark Ziegler | 1988–89 |
| Capt. Kevin Lauver, USMC | 1988–89 |
| Lt. Bruce Dillard | 1989–90 |
| LCdr. Doug McClain | 1988–90 |
| Maj. Chase Moseley, USMC | 1990 |
| *Capt. Pat Moneymaker | 1989–90 |
| Lt. Matt Seamon | 1989–91 |
| LCdr. Dave Inman | 1990–91 |
| LCdr. Lee Grawn | 1989–91 |
| LCdr. Randy Duhrkopf | 1991–92 |
| LCdr. John Foley | 1990–92 |
| LCdr. Pat Rainey | 1991–92 |
| Capt. Ken Switzer, USMC | 1991–93 |
| LCdr. Larry Packer | 1992–93 |
| *Capt. Greg Wooldridge | 1991–93 |
| Lt. Rob Surgeoner | 1993–94 |
| LCdr. Dave Stewart | 1992–94 |
| LCdr. Doug Thompson | 1992–94 |
| *Cdr. Bob Stumpf | 1993–94 |
| Lt. Tom Munson | 1995 |
| Lt. Ryan Scholl | 1995 |
| Lt. Mark Provo | 1995 |
| LCdr. Rick Young | 1993–95 |
| LCdr. Scott Anderson | 1993–95 |
| LCdr. Dave Kidwell | 1994–95 |
| Maj. Ben Hancock, USMC | 1994–95 |
| *Cdr. Donnie Cochran | 1986–88/95 |

Note: (*) indicates team leader.

## Maintenance Officers

| Name | Show Seasons |
|------|-------------|
| Lt. Bob Belt | 1949–50/52 |
| Lt. (j.g.) Bob Ittner | 1955–56 |
| LCdr. Harry Sonner | 1954–57 |
| LCdr. Bill Oleson | 1957–58 |
| Lt. (j.g.) Gus Kelley | 1958–59 |
| LCdr. Jack Reavis | 1959–61 |
| Lt. Ray Atherton | 1961–62 |
| LCdr. Scott Ross | 1963–65 |
| LCdr. Jack Gougar | 1966–67 |
| Cdr. Bud Jourden | 1968–69 |
| LCdr. Mac Prose | 1970–71 |
| LCdr. Fred Wiggins | 1972–74 |
| Lt. Mike Deeter | 1974–76 |
| Lt. Jack Johnson | 1977–78 |
| LCdr. Ben Woods | 1979–80 |
| LCdr. Al Edmonson | 1981–82 |
| Lt. Douglas Hill | 1983–84 |
| Lt. Jim Anderson | 1985–87 |
| Lt. Fred Cleveland | 1988–89 |
| Lt. Tom Schamberger | 1990–91 |
| Lt. Kevin Fischer | 1992–93 |
| Lt. Mark Evans | 1994–95 |

## Administrative Officers

| Name | Show Seasons |
|------|-------------|
| Lt. Mary Russell | 1969–70 |
| Lt. Bill Clark | 1977–80 |
| LCdr. Leo Boor | 1974–77/80–82 |
| Lt. Jim Proctor | 1983 |
| Lt. Hans Fett | 1984–86 |
| Lt. Jim Hawthorne | 1987–90 |
| CWO-4 Richard Marks | 1991 |
| LCdr. John Ottery | 1992–95 |

## Public Affairs Officers

| Name | Show Seasons |
|------|-------------|
| Lt. Morgan Smith | 1980–82 |
| LCdr. Douglas Schamp | 1983–85 |
| LCdr. Doug Hocking | 1986–87 |
| LCdr. Rusty Holmes | 1988–90 |
| LCdr. Chuck Franklin | 1991–92 |
| Lt. John Kirby | 1993–95 |

## Supply Officers

| Name | Show Seasons |
|---|---|
| Lt. Frank Grasso | 1980–82 |
| Lt. Vance Moore | 1983–85 |
| Lt. Sam Walker | 1986–88 |
| Lt. Greg Stroh | 1989–91 |
| Lt. Dismas Meehan | 1992–93 |
| LCdr. Rich Whelan | 1994–95 |

## Flight Surgeons

| Name | Show Seasons |
|---|---|
| LCdr. R.E. Luchars, MC | 1955–57 |
| LCdr. Bob Randolph, MC | 1974–75 |
| LCdr. Tim Peterson, MC | 1975–77 |
| Lt. Bernard Gipson, MC | 1977–79 |
| LCdr. Charles Thomason, MC | 1979–80 |
| LCdr. Kevin Wand, MC | 1981–82 |
| LCdr. Dwight Fulton, MC | 1983–85 |
| Lt. Wes Robinson, MC | 1986–88 |
| LCdr. Chuck Brady, MC | 1989–90 |
| LCdr. Pat Spruce, MC | 1991–92 |
| Lt. Perry Bechtle, MC | 1993–94 |
| LCdr. Andrew Nelson, MC | 1995 |

## Transport Pilots

| Name | Show Seasons |
|---|---|
| Maj. Lynn Jackson, USMC | 1954 |
| Capt. Ted Doyle, USMC | 1970–72 |
| Maj. John Garriott, USMC | 1970–72 |
| Maj. Anton Therriault, USMC | 1970–72 |
| 1st Lt. Joe Rodgers, USMC | 1972–74 |
| Capt. Al Coley, USMC | 1972–74 |
| Maj. Don Stiegman, USMC | 1972–74 |
| Capt. Ron Fleming, USMC | 1974–75 |
| Capt. Steve Petit, USMC | 1975–77 |
| Maj. Steve Murray, USMC | 1976–78 |
| Capt. Phil Brooks, USMC | 1976–78 |
| Capt. Bob Brandon, USMC | 1978–80 |
| Capt. Dan McConnell, USMC | 1978–80 |
| Capt. Chip Perrault, USMC | 1979–81 |
| Capt. Charlie Meyer, USMC | 1981 |
| Maj. Ken Hines, USMC | 1980–82 |
| Capt. "J" Joseph, USMC | 1982–84 |
| Capt. Ben Wyatt, USMC | 1983–85 |
| Capt. Stan Graham, USMC | 1985–86 |
| Capt. Peter Donato, USMC | 1983–86 |
| Capt. Mike Mullaly, USMC | 1986–87 |
| Capt. Mark Mykityshyn, USMC | 1987–88 |
| Maj. Frank Welborn, USMC | 1987–89 |
| Capt. Ken Hopper, USMC | 1988–90 |
| Maj. Rod Robinson, USMC | 1989–91 |
| Capt. Scott Larsen, USMC | 1990–92 |
| Capt. John Skinner, USMC | 1991–93 |
| Capt. Joe Michalek, USMC | 1992–94 |
| Capt. Stuart Smith, USMC | 1995 |
| Capt. Pat DeLong, USMC | 1994–95 |
| Capt. Craig Williams, USMC | 1993–95 |

# Index

A-4 Skyhawk, 53, 55, 61, 70, 95, 80, 92

Back-to-Back Pass, 57

C-130, 23, 75, 76, 116
Curtiss R5O-1, 41

Delta Landing, 61
Delta Roll, 107
Diamond Landing, 61
Diamond Loop, 23
Diamond Roll, 23, 42, 48
Dirty Loop, 73
Dutch Roll, 47

F-4 Phantom II, 55, 69, 70, 76, 76, 77, 95, 98
F/A-18 Hornet, 55, 93, 95, 97-99, 101, 104, 107,
    109, 115, 117
F6F Hellcat, 19
F7U-1 Cutlass, 34, 36, 37
F8F Bearcat, 17, 21, 25-27, 30, 31, 69
F9F-2 Panther, 27, 28

F9F-5 Panther, 33, 36, 47
F9F-6 Cougar, 41, 42, 45
F9F-8 Cougar, 45, 47, 51, 55
F9F-8T Cougar, 54
F11F Tiger, 51, 55, 61, 69
Fleur de Lis, 42, 88

Left Echelon Roll, 51, 97
Line-Abreast Loop, 50, 88, 97
C-121J Constellation, 65, 75

R4D-8 Super Skytrain, 41, 42
R5C-1, 42
R5D Skymaster, 65

TA-4J, 84
Three Flying Fish, 11
Three Sea Hawks, 10, 11, 115
Three T'Gallants'ls, 11
Tuckaway Cross, 97
Tuckover Roll, 97